A Statistic of One

A Statistic of One
My Walk with Glioblastoma Multiforme

By

Stephen Hatrak

iUniverse, Inc.
Bloomington

A Statistic of One
My Walk with Glioblastoma Multiforme

Copyright © 2012 by Stephen Hatrak.

All rights reserved. No part of this book may be used or reproduced by any means, graphic, electronic, or mechanical, including photocopying, recording, taping or by any information storage retrieval system without the written permission of the publisher except in the case of brief quotations embodied in critical articles and reviews.

"Scripture taken from the Holy Bible, New International Version Copyright @ 1973, 1978, 1984, by International Bible Society. Used by permission of Zondervan. All rights reserved."

"Scripture taken from the Message. Copyright @ 1993, 1994, 1995, 1996, 2000, 2001, 2002. Used by permission of NavPress Publishing Group."

iUniverse books may be ordered through booksellers or by contacting:

iUniverse
1663 Liberty Drive
Bloomington, IN 47403
www.iuniverse.com
1-800-Authors (1-800-288-4677)

Because of the dynamic nature of the Internet, any web addresses or links contained in this book may have changed since publication and may no longer be valid. The views expressed in this work are solely those of the author and do not necessarily reflect the views of the publisher, and the publisher hereby disclaims any responsibility for them.

Any people depicted in stock imagery provided by Thinkstock are models, and such images are being used for illustrative purposes only.
Certain stock imagery © Thinkstock.

ISBN: 978-1-4759-1634-8 (sc)
ISBN: 978-1-4759-1636-2 (hc)
ISBN: 978-1-4759-1635-5 (ebk)

Library of Congress Control Number: 2012907002

Printed in the United States of America

iUniverse rev. date: 05/04/2012

The easiest choice one can make is to quit, give up on themselves and their dreams; the only choice is to persevere through the bad times, laugh through the good times, and never quit on yourself through the in-between times.

Stephen Hatrak

DEDICATION

To Nancy, without your love in my life, your caring, understanding, respect and encouragement to live, laugh and love everyday, I would not be here today.

I want to thank the following people for their friendship.

Frances Bogdon
Bruce Blount

Preface

Throughout the book I hope to illustrate how my spirit, inner strength and faith were formidable allies on my journey with a glioblastoma. Before a single step was taken on my unexpected journey, I was who I was. Today, I am who I am.

While navigating the unknown terrain of my brain cancer, I had every reason to believe that my journey would bring me to the crossroads of new discoveries; I had no reason to believe that my life would continue as it had in the past, and that I would somehow emerge from this journey one in the same person. As human beings we are uniformly shaped by our experiences; past experience is no guarantee of what will happen or what we expect to happen in the future. The anxiety of facing what could be the ending of my life could have been unbearable if I allowed my suffering to be the focal point in my life. I had to shift my thoughts from death to living life while I lived; if not, it would diminish my will to move in the direction of healing and understanding.

Having a brain tumor did not stop the world around me from changing; everything and everyone is changing every minute of the day. When I awake in the morning I am not the same person from what I was the night before. As human beings, God has given us freewill and the ability to adapt to our changing environment and create better situations for ourselves.

If you look deeply into the phenomena of our existence we are a structure of four puzzle pieces; we are born, we live, grow old, and die. It is the universal foundation that God established for all human beings. On my journey, the obstacles I experienced challenged me how I would live my life with a diagnosis of glioblastoma. I had only two choices, I could either choose to control my life apart from my situation, or, be controlled by it. If I chose to let my situation control me and live life in its shadow, I would lose my center and thus my will to survive. It was logical to me that I must detach myself from a mindset of living in a shadow of death, if I was to move forward.

It was also important that I understand my world just as it is and not look to the past. The diagnosis of a high grade glioma tumor can create an ocean of suffering allowing moments that I could lose my direction and be swallowed up in an ocean of despair. How I navigated the surface of my diagnosis depended on what choices I made; I either succumb to my suffering, or let the strength of my inner spirit serve as my inspiration to do what I needed to do.

Throughout the book, I will be using selected passages from the Bible, which I felt offered an inspirational message to overcome the challenges that I believed would certainly present themselves on my journey with glioblastoma. The passages I have chosen are open to individual interpretation based on individual secular belief, as they should be; each individual will take away his or her own personal message to help cope with the trials that lay ahead of them. I invite you the reader to use the message of this book as a template for strengthening your inner spirit, never giving up on yourself, and always keeping your faith close to you.

Glioblastoma Multiforme

Glioblastoma Multiforme (GBM) is by far the most deadly of malignant brain tumors. Glioblastoma's do not discriminate when they intrude themselves into a person's brain. What I have witnessed, symptoms and signs effecting people with glioblastoma vary from individual to individual. My symptoms included: headaches, personality changes, and slowing of cognitive function. My headaches varied in intensity and were more severe in the morning upon first awakening, and the personality changes I had experienced varied in terms of my behavior, and were noticeable to everyone around me; my cognitive symptoms were mostly comprised of memory lapses, not being aware of my surroundings, and feeling like I was in a fog like state.

From what I was told when I was diagnosed, and, read over the past six years; generally speaking persons with the standard protocol of treatment that includes surgical resection, radiation therapy and chemotherapy, have a median survival of approximately 12 months. I suggest to the reader, however, that they do their own research regarding this topic to have available to them the latest statistics relative to the survival parameters of a glioblastoma diagnosis.

Cancer of any kind can be devastating; brain cancer brings its own special destruction. Our brain is the *Central Processing Unit* of our body; it is the core that establishes who you are, how you feel, the quality of your life, and a thousand of other minute functions.

Despite the dire statistics associated with a diagnosis of glioblastoma, there are several stories of long term survival; it is these stories that gave me hope that this cancer can be tamed. There are other stories to be told for those diagnosed with non-malignant brain tumors that can be equally as devastating, albeit death is not an imminent reality. A brain tumor of any kind will have its presence felt, and bring about effects on one's physical and cognitive functioning. One such story will be shared in the book.

INTRODUCTION

I never asked "why me." That question unfortunately has been asked by hundreds before me and it will remain one of life's mysteries for the ages.

The intent of this book is to share my walk with a diagnosis of Glioblastoma Multiforme, commonly referred to by the acronym *GBM*. My hope is, that you the reader will come away with the knowledge and enlightenment that despite the dire statistics of survival associated with glioblastoma, you think of yourself as I did a *statistic of one*. To overcome this challenge in my life, I had to believe in myself and leave the echoes of others behind me, and find that inner sixth sense within me to strengthen my resolve.

Living with a diagnosis of glioblastoma was frustrating at times; the trials that I had to overcome each day seem to last longer than I could imagine. What I had discovered is that we never know what obstacles God may throw our way as we travel our path in life; having a diagnosis of any form of cancer is certainly at the top. What encouraged me in these days of trials and tribulations was my faith. A scripture passage I read in the Bible, Jeremiah 29:11: "For I know the plans I have for you," declares the LORD, "plans to prosper you and not to harm you, plans to give you hope and a future", served as an inspirational message that God was always with me as I coped with my diagnosis.

Along the way, I had discovered several things about myself; I learned that life with brain cancer can be tough, but I am even tougher. The other, is what cancer cannot do . . . . separate me from my soul, squash my spirit, and stop the sun from rising in the east and setting in the west; creating new tomorrows and new opportunities.

For those of you reading this book who are diagnosed with glioblastoma; before you take your first step, don't ever give up the fight, and always reach for the light. I wish you Godspeed on your journey.

Chapter I

It is written that a journey of a thousand miles begins with the first step; my journey began on Saturday, February 25, 2006.

Although I was suffering for weeks with excruciating headaches, I continued to go to work as an Associate Administrator of a State Correctional Facility. I also continued to workout six days a week, golfed, and was planning to attend my first Polar Plunge to support the New Jersey Special Olympics on Sunday, February 26, 2006. As it turned out life had other plans for me.

Upon returning home from the gym on that fateful Saturday morning, I collapsed from the horrific pain I had been experiencing. How I managed to complete my workout and drive home is anyone's guess. A 911 phone call was made by my girlfriend Nancy, and moments later I found myself in the back of an ambulance and soon thereafter, I was in the emergency room at the local hospital. A cat scan of my brain was taken and what seemed like a lifetime, the doctor returned to my bedside and in a soft somber tone, told me that I had a tumor located in the right parietal region of my brain.

My immediate thought was that I was going to die. My Daughter, Marisa, was standing over my right shoulder at the time and I remember looking into her eyes and recalling how she ran into my arms when I would pick her up from her after school program when she was a young child. This recollection did not last long, as moments later I found myself in the back of another ambulance traveling to another hospital. Lying there, I asked myself is this the ending of my life? We all want that perfect ending and how it will unfold is anyone's guess. We will all have our own story to tell as we walk through life not knowing what is around every corner we turn. Life is an enigma wrapped in a mystery, a book with many chapters and by God's design we do not know the script that He has written for us. It is His plan that we move in His direction and do what He tells us.

After an overnight stay in ICU (Intensive Care Unit) I was moved to a bed in the main area of the hospital. On Sunday, the 26th, I first met with my neurosurgeon that was on call when I arrived at the hospital and we had a short conversation during which time he told me that I was "lucky," he was on call that day. (I would later learn that he was considered one of the top neurosurgeons in the tri-state area). Later that day, I was once again seen by the neurosurgeon who informed me that my operation (craniotomy) was scheduled for Wednesday, March 1st (Ash Wednesday). Prior to my surgery, I underwent a full body MRI to corroborate that the tumor was indeed a primary brain tumor and did not metastasis from another part of my body. I remember that day as if it were yesterday. I recall Nancy and my family by my side from the moment they gave me my pre-op sedative to the "stroll" to the operating room. I remember looking up at the ceiling, the fluorescent lights shining in my eyes, and musing to myself, is this what heaven will look like? As it would turn out, I would get a glimpse of heaven, which I will describe later in the book.

After several painstaking hours for my family and my girlfriend, the surgeon entered the waiting room and advised them that the operation was successful, (I would later learn that they were able to remove up to ninety percent of the tumor) and that it appeared I may have had a bout of *Multiple Sclerosis*, and years later I read that a glioblastoma can be disguised as Multiple Sclerosis. I began my post-op recovery in the intensive care unit and remember the room being dark, barely lit by the lights of the equipment monitoring my vital statistics, and I was still under the affects of the anesthesia, and in a dream like state. I remember lying there and hearing a male voice continuing to "bark" at me to breathe. The voice continued instructing me to breathe for several moments, whether I was having difficulty breathing or unable to breathe, I do not know. The following afternoon I was transferred back to my room from ICU where I continued my post-op recovery with intravenous doses of morphine for the pain, which was surprisingly tolerable and the steroid decadron for the swelling. The daily routine of taking blood samples through the day and night, along with frequent urine collections that I assumed were to ascertain if my kidneys were functioning properly, were a distraction to the ordeal of having my head cut open.

The following day Thursday, March 2nd I was seen by the neurosurgeon and he reiterated that the operation was successful, and that I could be going home as early as Friday, March 3rd. He also told me with a smile that when I awoke from the surgery in the operating room, it literally took four men to hold me down. I have a vague memory of that, I remember feeling like I was trapped in quicksand and could not breathe. I did not go home on Friday, because I felt uneasy leaving my comfort zone and was fatigued from the whole experience, and we thought it best that I remain in the hospital. Over the following days the routine was becoming so annoying that I couldn't wait to go home!

On Sunday, March 5th, I was discharged with a cotton cap and some seizure medication (Dilantin). Although I did not have a seizure prior to surgery, or after surgery, it was given as a precautionary measure. I was also given the steroid decadron for the swelling and some mild pain medication (I did not want the "hard stuff"). The ride home was comforting knowing that I would soon be in familiar surroundings, in my own bed, and not having intravenous lines of medication in my arms (24/7).

When I arrived home the first thing I did was to take off my cotton cap and look at my skull. What I saw was the "Frankstein Monster" without the electric bolts in my neck, and the staples holding my skull together, looking like a set of railroad tracks. It was hard for me to believe that this was really happening to me, and not just a bad dream that I would soon awake from.

The next several weeks were filled with colleagues, friends and family visiting me, and I was so surprised at the outpouring of "well wishes" by cards and telephone calls from so many people, some of whom I thought were ambivalent in their feelings towards me. Looking back, I am reminded of the moment when the lion received his heart from the *Wizard of Oz* and the wizard implied that a heart is not measured by how much you love, but rather how much you are loved by others. How true. At this time, I was on a regiment of medications (decadron and dilantin), which had to be given on a scheduled interval throughout the day and night over those first days home. I also noticed that the taste of metal was leaving a bad taste in my mouth, so I starting using plastic utensils. The only food that tasted good to me was peanut butter and jelly on a bagel and soup—that was my diet for days to come. These were not the only "changes" I would experience, and overtime, there would be more to come, as I will describe later.

The days turned into weeks, and before I knew it, Friday March 10th was here. I had been waiting for this day since I arrived home—my staples would be coming out! I had no idea what to expect, or what was about to happen next. Nancy and I arrived at the surgeon's office earlier than our scheduled appointment (we have a habit of being overly prompt). While we waited, I saw some of the people I encountered on the hospital floor where my bed was located. One in particular, was a young man, who had his girlfriend sleepover with him one night in his hospital bed, and I need not go any further, it was quite the night. What seemed like hours, we were finally called into the examination area.

When we entered one of the examining rooms, we were greeted by a nurse, who explained what the procedure would entail. The night prior to our appointment I had visions that the procedure would be like pulling staples from a stack of papers, and that vision was reinforced by the array of instruments I saw laid out on a table. Soon thereafter, the surgeon entered the room; I was seated on an examining table and swiped with antiseptic lotion, and the staples were removed one at a time. To my surprise, they were removed so effortlessly and with little or no discomfort. After their removal, I was once again swiped with lotion and asked to have a seat next to a table and chair while the surgeon stepped out for a moment. During this time my mind was wandering, still trying to comprehend what was happening. Everything still seemed so surreal to me, and I felt that I had no control over what was happening to me, and what would eventually be the final outcome to this madness. That feeling of having no control over your life was slowly sinking in.

Chapter II

When the surgeon re-entered, he stated that all looked well and that my tumor was an *Astrocytoma*. A what? I asked myself. Nancy and I both looked at each other for some type of clue (what we knew about brain tumors was equal to our knowledge of quantum physics). In an instant, we received the answer to our question when the surgeon went on to say that I would need to be seen by two additional doctors; as he wrote their names, each had their own specialty, and next to each name, was the word *oncologist*. That word I knew . . . . I looked at Nancy, and she at me, not a word was spoken; I felt like a sailboat racing in a regatta, and having all the wind sucked from my sails. Looking back, we should have asked so many questions that would have made sense, or brought clarity to what my situation was . . . . we were so naïve. After receiving the physician's names and telephone numbers he pretty much gave me a slap on the back, wished me luck, and scheduled another appointment to see him. I was so numb from the whole experience to this point that I felt like a trolley on a cable being pulled in either direction. When we arrived at our car, we began making appointments with the referred physician's.

My first scheduled appointment on Tuesday March 14th was with the radiation *oncologist*. Even though I knew "oncology" meant CANCER, I did not appreciate the seriousness of my situation. My thought was that people had cancer, and some survived as my Father had survived colon cancer. I would find out soon enough that "survival" was not a term loosely used for glioblastoma.

Soon after our arrival, I was given the standard information forms to fill out, and we found ourselves in an examination room. Too our surprise, the Doctor was already seated, and waiting (how often do you experience that). When we entered, he motioned for us to have a seat and asked succinctly, "do you know why you are here?" I replied, "I think so." He then went on to say that it appeared I had a Grade 3 or 4 malignant brain tumor. (The pathology report from the sample tumor was not available at the time of our visit, but would later reveal that I had glioblastoma multiforme), a grade IV malignant brain tumor. Still, these words were falling on deaf ears but the message was clear. I have a habit of wearing my prescription sunglasses even indoors and when he uttered those words, tears ran down my cheek. I then asked the inevitable question: "How long do I have?" His response, "I do not know I am not God." With that said I dried the tears on my cheek, put my sunglasses back on, and said "where do we go from here?" We scheduled an appointment for Tuesday, March 28th to begin my radiation treatment at the hospital. In the interim, I was scheduled to meet my medical oncologist on Thursday, March 23rd whose care I would be under for my chemotherapy treatment. At this time she discussed the role of chemotherapy in treating cancer and explained that the use of chemotherapeutic agents is to treat or prevent the recurrence of the cancer, and that these agents may be administered by various routes such as intravenously, orally, or locally, which involves the agents being injected or implanted directly into the tumor. She continued, stating that in general, chemotherapy is used at various points during the course of the disease. It can be used as the primary first line treatment and may be started immediately after the diagnosis, or, it can be used as a second form of treatment in addition to surgery or radiation. It also can be given before another type of primary therapy such as surgery or radiation therapy.

In my case, she said that the chemotherapy treatment is usually given after the tumor has been surgically removed in order to prevent recurrence of the tumor. She continued that there are a variety of chemotherapeutic options available for the treatment of glioblastoma, and the most commonly used was *temador*. She explained that this drug had become one of the most common agents used for glioblastoma. She continued that it was administered orally and that the major side effects associated with its use included nausea, fatigue, and myelosuppression of the bone marrow's ability to produce blood cells and platelets.

On Sunday, March 26th I began taking a small dose of temador along with my radiation treatments. In addition, I was given an anti nausea agent, and an antibiotic to fight off the risk of pneumonia while on chemotherapy. Throughout my treatment, I had to avoid being around anyone sick with flu type symptoms or even the common cold, and, to monitor my white blood count I would have a complete blood count (CBC) done with each visit to the medical oncologist (by the end of my treatment I felt like a human pin cushion).

At about this time I was now ready to begin my radiation therapy. When I met with the radiation oncologist he explained that radiation therapy represents the most effective treatment to surgery for the treatment of a glioblastoma. He then explained the two types of radiation protocols that would be used to treat me; the first, *Conventional Radiation* that uses radiation from an external source to destroy the cancer cells, and, that the primary goal of the radiation therapy after surgical removal of the brain tumor is to destroy residual cancer cells that cannot be removed by surgery, thereby, preventing or delaying recurrence of the tumor. (glioblastoma's have microscopic ventricles extending two or three centimeters beyond the discernable tumor boundaries.)

He continued that because high doses of radiation can also damage normal brain tissue, my radiation treatments would be divided into many smaller doses that would be administered over a period of 5 to 7 weeks. The other radiation to be used was Stereotactic Radiosurgery, and, that this therapy utilizes very accurately targeted high doses of radiation to destroy a tumor. He clarified that stereotactic radiosurgery was not actual "surgery" per se, but is a form of radiation therapy that enables doctors to destroy a brain tumor by accurately administering a single high dose of radiation in a one-day treatment session over a prescribed period of time. He went on to say that this therapy was commonly used for the treatment of inoperable brain tumors or recurrent brain tumors. He also said that this radiation therapy was also used for the treatment of secondary malignant brain tumors that spread to the brain from cancer in another part of the body known as *metastatic brain tumors*, but he felt that I should undergo this treatment as well.

My initial treatment began on Monday, March 27th, one day prior to my actual radiation therapy treatment. It began in a therapy radiation mould room; during this appointment, which lasted about thirty minutes, a thermoplastic mask was made of my head—this involved taking a flat piece of thermoplastic and warming it up in a warm water bath, it was then stretched over my face and head while I was lying down and I remember it felt like Jell-O to the touch. In about ten minutes or so, I could feel the plastic mush start to harden. Prior to the mask being made, I asked the technician what the mask would be used for, and the technician informed me that the mask would hold my head in position during each treatment. An hour or so after my "mask" was made; I had a CT scan with the mask on and these images, in addition to previous MRIs (Magnetic Resonance Imaging is a procedure that uses a magnet, radio waves, and a computer to make a series of detailed pictures of the brain and spinal cord) would be used by the radiation oncologist to develop a personalized treatment plan. In most cases of malignant brain tumors, a patient is injected with a substance called *gadolinium* into a vein; the gadolinium collects around the cancer cells so they show up brighter in the picture.

I began my conventional radiation therapy on Tuesday, March 28th and completed the therapy on May 1st. On May 2nd, I began my stereotactic radio surgery regiment. Prior to this the radiation oncologist informed me that some types of stereotactic radio surgery required a specially fitted mask or a frame attached to the scalp using small pins or anchors that go through the skin, to the surface of the skull or bone; luckily, I did not need to have a frame screwed onto my head.

On May 8th, I completed my stereotactic radio surgery treatment. Throughout my radiation treatments, fatigue was the most prominent side effect I experienced. The small dose of temador I was taking at this time also added to my fatigue. To help combat the fatigue I was drinking 8-10 glasses of non-caffeinated fluids (water); the water helped flush out the effects of the radiation. To keep up my energy I modified my workouts at the gym (yes, during my treatments I was able to work out at the gym). I modified my resistance training from one and a half hours to thirty minutes and also modified my cardio training from forty-five minutes to twenty minutes. This modified schedule combined with short naps of a half hour or so during the day helped me stay active throughout my treatments.

I did not experience any nausea or vomiting normally associated with radiation treatments, but was experiencing a mild numbness in my left foot. Throughout this time, I continued to take decadron to control brain swelling, and the side effects I experienced were swelling of my face, and some increase in my appetite, easy bruising, and some interference with my sleep. (I also experienced moments of agitation and hostility and regrettably it was often directed at Nancy. This was not a good experience for us.)

On May 12th, I was able to witness my Daughter, Marisa graduate college and was as proud as I could be. When this whole crazy ride began, I had my doubts I would be at this place in time. From that moment on, I never counted myself out, and all was possible: that was my mantra . . . . going forward.

At about this time I had my final visit with my neurosurgeon. He asked me how I was doing with my treatment, and told me that my MRIs were not "troubling" and that I should continue what I am doing, no more, no less. He advised me to "take it easy" at the gym and not to lift heavy weight so as not to put any extra pressure on my brain because I still had some swelling. He also said to make sure that I continue the decadron, despite the side effects I was experiencing. I replied that I did modify my workout significantly and I also advised him that there were many times I would make contact with a stray piece of equipment, which would cause me to bleed profusely. He explained that this was due to one of the side effects of the decadron. He cautioned me to be extra careful in and out of the gym. (After having two occasions of this happening, a first aid kit became a permanent staple of my gym bag.)

Prior to leaving I asked him about driving. He told me that since I had no history of seizures prior to or after surgery, driving should be no problem so long as I kept within a 10 mile radius (the gym and the golf course were almost exactly that distance.) He also told me that this could change depending on any changes in my condition, and, that this would be a judgment call by my doctor's. This was the last time I saw him. He eventually took a position with a hospital in the State of Texas.

Two weeks later, I met with my radiation oncologist. I told him I was feeling better than expected and that if not for routine MRIs (every other month) the medications and doctor office visits, I would never know I was "sick." I advised him of the numbness I was feeling in my left foot, and he made no comment, just a note in my chart (what I have learned is that you must be your own advocate and ask as many questions as you need to ask to gain clarity on what you are experiencing and your treatment. This is something I would do as I continued to move forward.)

The following day, I met with my medical oncologist to discuss my chemotherapy treatment plan now that I was off radiation treatments. She advised me that my dosage would be increased from the dosage I was on during my radiation treatments and that I would begin my first cycle on June 9th.

During this time, I was driving, working out at the gym and playing golf, so I decided that perhaps it was time for me to go back to work. Nancy urged me to wait for a while longer, but I was determined (looking back, I should have listened.) On June 2nd, I met with my Division Director and the Commissioner. The meeting went very well and they gave me their "ok." I was able to set my own schedule which I worked out with the Administrator of the Correctional Facility where I was employed as the Associate Administrator. I would begin working half days, Monday through Friday. When I arrived on my first day, many of my colleagues asked "what are you doing here?" They later told me that they were really not surprised since I rarely took time off in my career, other than scheduled vacation days. The first week was a little straining and I had difficulty absorbing information "and staying on point." So I decided to give the most cognitive tasking responsibilities of my position to one of the Assistant Superintendents. I also began my first cycle of chemotherapy with the higher dose around this time. It wasn't long before I knew that no matter how much I wanted to have everything "back to normal" in my life, work was the missing piece. It wasn't going to be, by June 16th, after two weeks of returning to work, it was over. I said my goodbye's, thanked everyone for their support, and walked out the door. I would visit the facility on occasion, over the following months.

Days later, I celebrated Father's Day with my Daughter and my family. No one paid any extra attention to me which was a good thing. I did not need to see solemn faces and everyone walking on "egg shells" to remind me what I was walking around with, nor, to be the focus of any additional attention. The following months were filled with doctor appointments, leaving little or no time to reflect on my life as it was and now as it is.

During the month of August, I went to a scheduled appointment I had made to see an orthopedic physician about my left foot. The numbness was not going away but seemed to be worsening, something I advised my radiation oncologist of at every appointment, but only received vague explanations. It seemed as though it wasn't something I should be concerned with, so I did not persist any further. The X-rays taken of my foot and ankle taken by the orthopedic physician did not reveal any type of arthritis or other issues. During another routine appointment with the radiation oncologist, I again brought up the increasing numbness in my left foot, and, that I was seen by an orthopedic physician days earlier, which shed no light on the matter either. He told me that solely on what I was reporting, that I was probably experiencing some mild nerve damage due to the chemotherapy treatments, and, that it could possibly dissipate over time so I did not press any further, and made a note to speak with the medical oncologist about this.

During the month of October, Nancy and I participated in a 5k walk a friend from the gym was sponsoring for a local police officer who passed away from cancer. Despite the numbness in my left foot, I was able to complete the walk, along with Nancy and the aid of a cane. I also met with both my medical, and radiation oncologist's to go over my seizure medication and their approval for reinstating my driving privileges with the Division of Motor Vehicles. In an earlier visit to the medical oncologist, I had experienced a small hand tremor which she perceived to be a seizure. Inasmuch, she was bound by law to report this to the Division of Motor Vehicles resulting in my driving privileges being revoked, pending a certification from her that I could operate a motor vehicle safely. Over a period of time, she did complete the required certification and my driving privileges were restored.

On November 13th, I reached the day that I believed was impossible to reach when I was first diagnosed, it was my 53rd birthday. I celebrated the day with Nancy with little or no fanfare (We did not want to bring more attention to this birthday than any other birthday).

On December 25th, I celebrated Christmas Day with Nancy and my family and I had so much to be thankful for. I celebrated with rejuvenation in my faith. Like me, and others, I am sure diagnosed with glioblastoma initially believe that there is no end in sight. During the course of our journey, we somehow find our way back to our faith for comfort and hope.

The year was coming to an end and what I experienced over the past year left me with a sense of grit and determination to face the challenges that may appear on my horizon moving forward; and that no matter what happened in the past and what may happen in my future was of little consequence if I continued to rely on my inner spirit to move forward, and live life to its fullest, and continue to take each step no matter how small and appreciate the tomorrows made for me; the Lord is my light and my salvation—whom shall I fear? The Lord is the stronghold of my life—of whom shall I be afraid? (Psalms 27:1)

Chapter III

On January 1, 2007, Nancy and I began our tradition of going to the beach on New Year's Day. Afterwards, we spent the day quietly at home and looked back over the year and wondered what would lie ahead of us. We didn't dwell too long on this; we were resigned to the fact that what will be, will be. The following day, I met with a neurologist that I had added to my treatment team for a routine follow-up visit. I had discussed this with my medical oncologist and she was in favor of it too, since she had no significant practice in the field of neurology, and thought it would be a compliment to my treatment plan. I continued on my chemotherapy with no complications, other than the increasing numbness in my left foot.

On January 26th, Nancy and I registered for a polar plunge event in Seaside Heights, the same event I missed in February 2006. On February 24th, we attended the event along with some friends from the gym and although I could not actually participate in the event, it was good to be there.

On March 1st, I "celebrated" one year of living with glioblastoma (I use March 1st as my anniversary date because that was the day of my operation.) I was still feeling good both physically and psychologically given my diagnosis, and was still playing golf and working out at the gym. My ability to walk was still a little "shaky," but the use of a cane for long distances did the trick. My MRIs continued to show no signs of a recurring tumor or new tumor growth, and the edema (swelling) also appeared to be diminishing and the tumor had also decreased in size.

As I entered my second year of "survival," and I use this word loosely as I mentioned earlier, due to the fact that survival is not a word frequently used when referring to glioblastoma. When I was first diagnosed it was inferred that my survival would not be measured in years, but rather in months. When I went on the Internet to research the cancer that invaded my brain, it pretty much corroborated what my doctors inferred, instead of survival, the piece I was reading used the words *prolonging life* when it came to glioblastoma. I was so convinced that I would die within months of my diagnosis, I actually went out and bought a crypt in a mausoleum, and to this date, I still have the deed tucked away in a drawer. I sometimes look at this deed when I am rummaging through the desk drawer looking for a pen or something, and smile, and muse to myself that the statistics used to ascertain my longevity are nothing more than numbers, they do not have a pulse, and they do not have feelings, a soul, or a spirit. These are qualities that I have as a human being and it is these qualities, in every individual, that make them their own success story. It is God's job to let us know when it is time to come home.

Believing that death was right around the corner I cannot tell you how many times I cried like a little child while waiting in the parking lot for the gym to open. I was safe to share these feelings with myself, in private, at 4:30 a.m. in the morning since the gym opened at 5:00 a.m. While listening to the radio, songs from my past brought back memories of what used to be. I thought frequently of my daughter, and who would be there to hold her hand when she needed reassurance, to lean on when times got rough, to dry her tears when she was upset, and to walk her down the aisle on her wedding day. The tears would just flow. I also thought about Nancy. I think sometimes the person left behind has the worst of it and I know that if I lost my daughter or Nancy, it would be almost unbearable. As the time got closer to 5:00 a.m., and the parking lot began to fill with cars, it was my cue to wipe the tears and get on. This scenario would continue off and on for the time I would allow it. Moments like this are good for the soul so long as I did not dwell too long in this "house of despair" and lose sight of living life while I lived. The easiest choice I could have made was to quit, quit on myself and my dreams; the only choice to make was to challenge myself through the bad times, laugh through the good times, and never give up through the in between times.

Moving on to March, I met with my medical oncologist for a routine visit. Everything was going well and I was tolerating the temador, but was still experiencing the numbness in my left foot, this, along with the constipation were the only problems I was having. I was able to play golf on a few occasions and it was fascinating to my friends that I was able to take my chemo, orally, while waiting for our "tee time" to be called. Spring was here and in full bloom. I celebrated two of my sister's birthday's along with my family (I have two sets of twin sisters and an older sister) yes, no brothers. I again met with my medical oncologist for a routine follow-up visit and met with my neurologist to discuss my seizure medication (*keppra.*) The dosage he had me on was just too high—I was feeling much too tired and found myself sleeping more than I liked, and he agreed to lower the dosage. I also met with the radiation oncologist and since my MRIs were not showing any "severe" swelling and had just about dissipated, I asked if I could now come off the decadron. It was decided I could start weaning off the steroid, and what a relief it was to me. I wanted my old face back; I was tired of my face looking like a helium filled "party balloon." The only thing that was missing to complete the picture was some sparkles and a ribbon string tied around my neck. This would be my last appointment with him, and before I left I said to him that I would be celebrating 2 years of "survival" soon, he looked at me with a puzzling look and a shrug as if he knew that was against all odds. I felt like I was losing a friend, he had been with me since the beginning. I later learned that he had taken a position in a New York Hospital.

The month of May began with visits to my doctors for routine follow-ups. I was able to play a few rounds of golf and spend some time outdoors. At this time I noticed some subtle changes in my motor skill functioning (eye-hand coordination) and moving my left side in sync with my right side; necessary movements to complete the golf swing, lift weights in correct form, and swim. June finally arrived and I was tired of the cold, semi-cold weather, we were experiencing for the month of May. Nancy and I were looking forward to spending time at the beach; we always enjoyed the beach, and were often referred to as "beach bums." We enjoyed long walks, soaking up the sun and for me, body surfing. Even though I was unable to swim or walk due to the numbness and mild coordination problems, I still enjoyed the atmosphere the beach provided.

I continued with my chemotherapy treatment and had an overall sense of well-being despite the cancer and its effects. My MRI showed that my tumor had decreased in size. The combination treatment of radiation and chemotherapy appeared to be working its way to eradicate the tumor.

Overall, July was a good month, except for the realization that my golfing days may soon be at an end. I am not one to easily give up on anything, I taught myself to golf by practicing in fields and playing golf with Nancy on executive courses; it was Nancy who introduced me to golf, it wasn't pretty, but anything worth pursuing requires hard work and perseverance. Prior to a round of golf with my friends, I noticed I was having trouble holding my clubs and I was now experiencing some numbness in my left hand and leg, which was making it harder for me stand for a long period of time.

By the end of July, I could no longer participate in golf. On a perfectly glorious Sunday, lower temps and humidity for this time of year, my friends and I would be playing our favorite course. As we were waiting for the group ahead of us to clear the fairway the numbing sensation that I was experiencing was becoming more intense. I also noticed on practice swings I was having difficulty coordinating the motion of a golf swing. When our group came to hit our "tee shots," I made several unsuccessful attempts to strike the ball, and on my last attempt I hit a so-so drive. I approached my ball just outside the fairway in the "short rough," and two shots later I found myself in a green-side bunker, several attempts later, I found the "green." But the fluid, coordinated motion of a golf swing was still not there, and I had trouble standing over the ball as I was getting ready to "putt."

As we approached the second "tee," I was having a difficult time and when I went to place the "tee" in the ground, at the second tee box, I could barely maintain my balance. After several missed attempts at striking the ball, I hit a marvelous drive, long, and in the middle of the fairway. As I approached the ball and then positioned myself over it, I missed the ball several times. My friends were very understanding, but, I was holding them up (golf is a game of rhythm.) It was obvious to all without a word being said, that this would be a long frustrating round if I continued, and it was too beautiful a day to watch me "hack" at the ball all afternoon. Not wanting to ruin their day, I picked up my ball, said goodbye, and walked back to the clubhouse. That was my last day; losing the ability to participate in golf would be one of the many things I would come to lose on this unexpected journey.

As I entered the month of August, my chemotherapy treatments continued, as well as my bi-monthly MRI. At this time I was introduced to a new radiation oncologist, who I had previously met during my initial radiation treatments. My first impression of him at that time was a man with an alpha personality, and a "stuffed shirt" who thought much of himself. I am also an alpha personality, and knew it was going to make for a "dicey" relationship, and that time would tell. Nancy and I were able to go to the beach several times and enjoy the serenity of the ocean. My scheduled MRI once again showed that my tumor had decreased in size. This gave Nancy and me a sense of hope that perhaps I might make it for another few months.

On Saturday, September 1st, I reached the 18 month mark of living with this cancer that invited itself into my life. The following weeks consisted of a routine month of chemotherapy, and the need to make an appointment with a gastroenterologist. This doctor had previously treated me in 1994, for a gastrointestinal problem, and, I had no reoccurrence of this until this time; whether it was brought on by the radiation and/or chemotherapy treatments was not discussed.

October arrived, and the cooler weather was a relief to the late summer heat and humidity. I was enjoying watching my favorite college football team (Notre Dame), and my favorite pro-team (Philadelphia Eagles). My days were filled with follow-up appointments with my doctor's, and working out at the gym, although somewhat limited. I also had my MRI which once again showed a decrease in the tumor. Nancy and I also attended another 5k walk/run sponsored by a friend of ours and we were planning on attending the "Have a Chance" walk to fight brain cancer in New York's Battery Park with my sister Lisa, and her boyfriend. I was not having a good week leading up to the event, and was unfortunately unable to attend. I also experienced a new wrinkle to the "quality" of my life. I often tell people that "quality of life" is not measured by what you can and cannot do, but measured by how you choose to live life while you live. Over the past several months my ability to walk had deteriorated, and the numbness that I was experiencing in my left foot had progressed to my left leg, making walking more difficult. The need for a cane to walk distances of more than a hundred yards or so, was now a necessary part of my life; short distances were still available to me that enabled me to continue at the gym somewhat unimpeded. However, I knew a decision would have to be made in the near future regarding some type of motorized scooter, or at the minimum a wheelchair, if I wanted to stay engaged in life; I needed to adapt to my situation so Nancy and I could still enjoy going to outdoor flea markets and "strolling" on the boardwalk. In everyone's life there comes a time when they have to adapt to changes in their environment, whether it be in their professional or personal lives, or dealing with an aspect of their health. It was this ability to reset myself that would determine my quality of life; I could either decide to sit on the sidelines and watch life pass me by, or jump in the game.

On November 13th, I celebrated my 54th birthday; another day to be thankful for and another month of appointments, and chemotherapy—I will take these "dull" routine months any time. We celebrated Thanksgiving with a lot to be thankful for.

My December MRI once again showed a decrease in the tumor, and we celebrated Christmas with much to be grateful for; it was a celebration of Jesus' birth and the continued "rebirth" of me. We all too often, lose the message of Christmas, we get caught up in the festivities surrounding Christmas, receiving gifts and spending time with family and friends; and we may even make that symbolic visit to church. Christmas, is about love, moments of sharing the spirit of Jesus' birth and the warm feeling it brings to us, sharing the spirit amongst us, and should not be delegated to a single date on the calendar; this is something we should strive to achieve everyday. Our faith is the foundation of our spiritual existence, and we often take for granted the tomorrows that we receive, and fool ourselves into believing that we alone can save ourselves from the frailties of life. Christmas, presents us with the opportunity to reach deep into our heart, and share the spirit of love, and connect with the true essence of the nativity. I believe the scripture passage Corinthians I 13:4 describes this best:

> Love is patient, love is kind.
> It does not envy, it does not boast,
> it is not proud, it is not rude,
> it is not self serving, it is not easily angered,
> it keeps no record of wrongs.
> Love does not delight in evil,
> but rejoices with the truth.
> It always protects, always trusts and always hopes,
> always perseveres.

Chapter IV

January 1, 2008, and yet another year lies ahead of me with new opportunities, and I am sure new challenges to overcome. Looking back over the past two years of my life it was hard to believe everything Nancy and I went through, and yet here we stood, moving forward together, united in our faith and love for one another.

Going through a time in my life when living and dying was a crapshoot, it was not surprising that I saw the world from a different point of view; I stepped to the beat of my own drum, and there were many times when that drum beat an extra step while battling this terrible cancer. Over time, I discovered my inner "sixth sense" to help me navigate the anxiety and fear associated with a glioblastoma diagnosis, and the challenges that would ultimately face me. I knew to accomplish this, I must face my fears and challenge myself to overcome the changes brought about by my diagnosis, and not be fearful of what lays ahead of me as I continued to challenge myself to live life on my terms.

February arrived with very cold and wintry conditions. The cold weather seemed to be having an unusual effect on me that I never experienced prior to my diagnosis, and I was also now very sensitive to contact with my body if it were done without my knowledge. I remember an incident that happened one day while Nancy and I were shopping at the local Acme Supermarket, a friend of the family who I had not seen for years, came up from behind me and grabbed my arm; I instinctively turned toward her, and pulled away from her. I was embarrassed, and saw the look of shock on her face, and explained to her about my medical condition which she was unaware of. We both apologized to one another and continued with our shopping. At about this time, we attended a Brain Tumor Support Group meeting located forty miles east of us. The group's co-founder is a strong determined woman deeply devoted to bringing brain tumor awareness to the forefront of the community at large, and is also a brain tumor survivor of fifteen plus years. She is joined by a sidekick who helps facilitate the meeting, who is also a brain tumor survivor of multiple years. We were both surprised at the number of people there; we thought having a brain tumor was an occurrence not affecting many people, and also discovered that not all brain tumors are cancerous.

I would say that of the members there, more than a few were effected with a malignant brain tumor such as mine. It was interesting to hear that most of those effected with a non-malignant tumor had survived up to 15 years and counting. To the "novice," this number could be deceiving considering the median survival rate for glioblastoma. Later in the book I will write more about our experiences with the support group, the people we met, and the people we lost along the way.

During my adult life I was not an overly religious man, and I did not attend church on a regular basis, and was not always true to my faith. As a young boy in the 5th grade, I was chosen, along with other boys' (girls at that time were not considered) to be an *altar boy*. Parts of the Mass were still conducted in Latin, and required us to read and speak our parts in Latin (a year or so later, those parts were said in English.) At the time I felt it was an honor to be chosen, and what criterion was used to select me I do not recall? Throughout my tenure up to the eighth grade, I participated in many Masses, wedding ceremonies and funerals. Looking back, I sometimes believed I was being called upon to serve God in a special way. It was at this time, I was approached by a Nun, Sister Mary Claire, and from what I remember she was in her early twenties and her face was a picture of beauty. The purpose of her coming to see me was to start a chapter of the *Saint Dominic Savio Club* at the school. I embraced this request with enthusiasm; perhaps my enthusiasm was inspired because I enjoyed her company. We met several times and began a study group with other students. Halfway through the establishment of the group, she was transferred to another parish, and I, was months away from graduating and my participation would come to an end. If the club continued I do not know. To this date, I wonder sometimes if I missed my "calling."

During my lifetime, I had two visits with my *guardian angel*. My first visit with my *guardian angel* occurred in late March, 1984. My daughter, Marisa was due to be born in early April and I remember one night, I had been praying when I first retired for the evening; I was praying to God that He bless me with a baby girl. I know most men would like a son, but I knew in my "heart of hearts," I would be a much better father to a daughter. It seemed as though I just fell into a deep sleep, when I felt a presence surrounding me. It wasn't frightening, but a calming sensation, like a soft wind across your face. There was a scent in the room that I was not familiar; it smelled sweet, but had a somewhat bitter aftereffect in the nostrils.

What happened next was just as peculiar—in the corner of the room was an illuminating light; engulfed in this light was what I believed to be the shape of a woman—she had long golden hair, was wrapped in white clothing, and clutched some sort of book in her hand. Above her head was an orb, just as bright as the light surrounding her. At the tip of her shoulders was an object protruding from her side, and it appeared to be a feather like piece of clothing; I could not stare too long, because the light was sensitive to my eyes—similar to staring into a bright sunlight. In an instant, the figure spoke in a strange dialect, but I understood what the woman said to me: "God has heard your prayers, and you will have a daughter; protect her, nourish her, and be righteous in your teachings." With that, the image was gone. I will never forget that night, and three days later my daughter, Marisa was born.

My second visitation came on a February night that was not a particularly good night for me. I was in pain and discomfort, and it was difficult to rest never mind sleep. As I looked around the room I settled in and I began to pray. I prayed that *Mother God* place her hands on my head and take away the cancer that had invaded my brain, and, that if it were God's will that I survive so let it be; if not, I give my soul to Him without reservation. What seemed like forever, I finally fell to sleep (I think) with the thought of my prayer.

As what occurred in 1984 I once again felt a presence in the room. A bittersweet aroma filled the room, and standing beside me was a female figure drenched in a luminous light. Her hair was a golden brown, she was dressed in white with a blue flock; she extended her hand towards me and her smile was so comforting. As I extended my hand I could not feel her hand in mine. In a nanosecond, I was standing in a pasture. The grass was so green, there were flowers in all shapes and colors; colors so bright that they cast shadows. There were trees dotting the landscape with leaves that seemed to dance from the tree's limbs; they too were all shapes, and bright in color. There was a silence as if I were in a tunnel; the sky was so blue and seemed to be endless. The clouds were illuminating and appeared to be extending beyond what the naked eye could see. It was the most beautiful sight one could imagine; all the time the "lady" was by my side.

I came along what appeared to be a bank surrounding a river and seated along the bank were "*people*." There were others walking along the bank where I stood with the "lady" and they were dressed in white gown like garments, and had long flowing white/gray hair, and they seemed to communicate without speaking. From the moment I arrived, any pain I was experiencing vanished instantly. It was so peaceful. As I was acclimating myself to the surroundings, the "lady" extended her hand, I did not want to take it, and I did not want to leave. She smiled at me and touched my shoulder and whispered in a dialect unfamiliar to me, yet again, I understood every word: "It is not your time." Instantly I found myself in my bed, wet with perspiration as if I had jumped into a river.

My MRI in February once again showed a decrease in the tumor. During this month we attended another polar plunge event in Seaside, New Jersey to support the Special Olympics. It was nice being among the hundreds of participants, among them, some friends from the gym who I had not seen since the last event. Although I could not participate, it meant a lot to me to be there. It was two years ago, almost to the date I was taken to the hospital and diagnosed with a brain tumor.

The polar plunge events will forever be a reminder of the "beginning" of my new life . . . . I lost my former self in the cold waters of the Atlantic ocean that February in 2006, and even though I was not there physically, I do believe that my spirit was, and continues, to ride the changing tides that wash my spirit back onto the shore, to live yet another day. Whenever I visit the beach I look to the ocean for the answers I seek. The ocean will always be a symbolic piece of my spirit, and at these times, I recall the account of creation in the Bible scripture (Genesis 1:1-27) and see the miracles that God created for me. Throughout my journey, I accepted God into my life and came to the realization that God would always be with me through the changes in my life. Change, is never easy, and sometimes seems impossible to overcome; there were times that I questioned my faith, and asked why God allows such suffering. I was reminded of a Bible verse: Therefore my heart is glad and my tongue rejoices; my body also will rest secure, because you will not abandon me to the realm of the dead, nor will you let your faithful one see decay. You make known to me the path of life; you will fill me with joy in your presence, with eternal pleasures at your right hand. (Psalms 16:9-11)

Chapter V

On March 1st, I reached the unthinkable; two years of living with the deadliest of malignant primary brain tumors. Despite my MRIs showing a consistent decrease in my tumor, I remained cautiously optimistic about my chance to survive much more beyond this. I was continuing my chemotherapy treatments along with a regiment of reflexology (whether it was a coincidence or not, when Nancy began performing reflexology, my tumor began to steadily decline in size.) During the course of anyone's journey with a terminal illness they will discover what they believe is their own *silver bullet* to combat their illness. Just as we are a "statistic of one" in terms of our survival, anything we believe that works for us is a good thing . . . . whatever gets you through the night.

I was also now nearing the two year recommended threshold to remain on temador, and was discussing when I would stop my chemotherapy with my medical oncologist. We never got the chance, to follow up on this conversation, because, at this time I felt the need to now make a change in oncology care. As I mentioned earlier, the medical oncologist was not versed in neurology which she readily admitted. During a visit with my parents, my Mom told me of a conversation she had with a doctor at the hospital where she volunteered, and had mentioned to him that I had glioblastoma, and to her surprise, he told her that his Mother was being treated for the same condition by a local *neurooncologist*. (Neurooncology is the field of specialization dealing with tumors of the central nervous system.) After discussing this with Nancy, I made the decision to transfer my care to this doctor. I did not see my medical oncologist to tell her of this decision, instead, I called her office and left a message thanking her and her staff for the awesome care they gave me, and how much I appreciated their efforts. To this day I regret that decision—I owed her and her staff an in-person "thank you" and years later Nancy and I would encounter one of the nurses at a cancer survival event at the hospital—I took that opportunity, to hug and thank her, and everyone involved in the early days of my diagnosis for the care they gave me.

Before I met with the neurooncologist, I was asked, prior to the appointment, to bring all my records and my MRIs up to this time. The meeting went well as could be expected. Nancy and I were both somewhat comfortable with him. We discussed my case and stopping my chemotherapy treatment. At about this time, I had my scheduled MRI and once again the tumor had decreased in size. On April 8th we celebrated my daughter's 24th birthday. Every birthday was always a special time for me, even more so now.

On my next visit with the neurooncologist we discussed my chemotherapy treatment, and it was decided that I would take my last dose of temador at the end of this month's cycle. My treatments had become a constant and comforting part of my life, and setting aside my "crutch" would be a bittersweet moment. I asked myself, would I die when I stopped my chemotherapy treatment? Like a car's engine needing gasoline to run, did I need temador running through my engine to make me run? The decision to terminate my chemotherapy was ultimately based on the recommended time frame of up to two years.

All along, up to this point in time, I continued resting and acclimating myself to the "new me." There were still many times when I looked in the mirror and did not recognize the face starring back at me, and, I was now also reading as much as I could. I always enjoyed reading books of a historical nature; however, reading such books was now a time consuming chore; keeping dates and facts straight was difficult, as well as comprehending what I was reading. I often had to reread passages and even entire chapters. Prior to my diagnosis, reading was a delightful way to spend a lazy afternoon, and now it was a reminder of what I was once able to enjoy. Even so, it did not stop me. While "surfing" through a magazine, I came across an article that suggested succeeding at any challenge in life takes courage and trusting your instincts, that inner voice that charts your course. I used that as a template when contemplating the decisions I would have to make to continue living life, and realizing that yesterday was yesterday and today is today.

In May, we attended another support group meeting and were acclimating ourselves to the surroundings and getting to know some of the members a little better—we no longer felt like "outsiders." At the first meeting we attended, we mostly kept to ourselves. The majority of the members were from the Monmouth/Ocean County area. Over time the spirit of togetherness brought us closer to the group and other than that, May turned out to be a routine month. By this time, I had few doctor appointments, and other than my keppra I was not taking any "brain cancer" related medication and it felt good.

June arrived with no new problems, other than the numbness in my left side which was now progressing upwards my left leg and left arm, but, not enough to cause concern, but enough to cause discomfort. I had my routine scheduled MRI and once again the tumor had decreased in size.

A few days later, I awoke feeling extremely lightheaded and unable to keep my balance, and I could not walk more than a few feet without tumbling. Everything around me was spinning and I had no control over my body, my first thought was, "this can't be happening," I just had my MRI which did not detect any new problems or concerns, still, not taking any chances, off we went to the Emergency Room. Hours later (if you ever had the pleasure of going to an emergency room, you know what I am talking about) a decision was made to keep me overnight for observation. Fearing what I was experiencing was related to my brain cancer, I insisted to be taken to the hospital where my neurooncologist was affiliated since his practice was located in Ocean County, and, he did not have standing in my local hospital. A telephone call was made and I was transferred that day. Upon my arrival I was met by a nurse and escorted to my room, and sometime later I was seen by my neurooncologist. He did not appear to be overly concerned, since my MRI did not show anything that could possibly cause these symptoms. I was put on some intravenously administered medications and kept overnight into Saturday. On Sunday, I was released and returned home. Before leaving the hospital, my doctor believed that the ER staff overreacted to my condition based upon my underlying brain cancer. (I think I did too—but hey, who wouldn't.) He said that it appeared what I had experienced was vertigo, and, that the medication I was receiving was *antivert* to combat the symptoms. I felt much better knowing things were "ok in the ole brain."

Over the next few days, Nancy and I were able to go to the shore and "soak up the sun" for a few hours despite the fact that I was still experiencing some digestive problems. July was here before we knew it, and with it, another a new *wrinkle* to deal with. I met with my neurooncologist for a routine office visit, and I advised him of the increased numbness I was experiencing, but other than that and my digestive issues things were "ok." He explained that the numbness I was experiencing was probably due to some nerve damage from my chemotherapy treatments. At this point in time, I had been off chemotherapy for three months. We agreed to monitor the progression of the numbness on my left side, thinking that it may subside over time. I had also, over the past several weeks, been experiencing pain in my pelvic area and lower abdominals, so I made an appointment with my family doctor. Despite the cancer, I was still prone to the everyday maladies of life and growing older.

During the examination it was believed the problem was with my bladder. I was referred to an urologist for follow-up. My first two appointments were unremarkable. On both occasions, the urologist also believed I was having a problem with my bladder, since I was having pain <u>after</u> urination—apparently a sign of bladder pain which is why, I was experiencing the pain in my lower abdominals and pelvic area. This diagnosis was made without a procedure being performed. He did however; draw blood for a *prostate specific antigen* (PSA). The (PSA) results showed a mild enlargement of the prostate consistent with my age, which did not cause for any alarm. He casually said that there was a procedure that could be performed, but, he seemed hesitant due to what I believe was my cancer diagnosis. He prescribed bladder pain medication, and scheduled a follow-up appointment six months out.

August arrived and it was hotter and more humid than I could remember. I had my scheduled MRI, and, once again the tumor decreased in size. Other than seeing the dentist for a routine cleaning, I spent most of my time resting and staying out of the heat. We were able to go to the beach just once; the heat really bothered me, and it was difficult to sit for a long period of time, due to the nerve damage I was experiencing. September finally brought some relief to the August heat and humidity and the month was a quiet one; I could get used to this, I thought. I was now five months off my chemotherapy treatments and based on my MRI results it would appear that my treatments were keeping the cancer at bey. I tried not to get ahead of myself, but it felt good to believe that I may make it to three years. Positive thinking is good for the soul, so long as I differentiated between hopes and expectations. I believe that hopes and expectations have a distinct difference in terms of what we hope and expect from life when terminal cancer is part of your every day existence.

I also, met with my neurooncologist on a routinely scheduled visit, and he was extremely pleased with my results thus far, and even suggested that I could be in this for the "long haul;" based on prevailing statistics—there are those damn statistics again which I have chose to ignore months after my initial diagnosis, and concentrate on only one statistic—me. During our visit, I mentioned once again, that the numbness I was experiencing from the very beginning was now progressing thru my left arm, and that my entire left side was now under siege. Before I could continue, he suggested to me that I was most likely suffering from *peripheral neuropathy* due to the *cytotoxicity* of the chemotherapy; although temador is not known to have this side effect associated with its use, he explained to me that peripheral neuropathy by definition, is a result of nerve damage and often causes numbness and pain in your hands and feet, he suggested that in many cases symptoms improve with time. I then asked, "What exactly is peripheral neuropathy?" He stated that the peripheral nervous system sends information from your brain and spinal cord (central nervous system) to all other parts of the body and back again. He continued, nerves that may be affected included: Sensory nerves that receive sensations such as heat, pain or touch; motor nerves that control how your muscles move; and autonomic nerves that control functions such as blood pressure, heart rate, digestion and bladder function. At the conclusion of my visit, I thought how the gradual onset of numbness that began in my left foot, and now had spread upward to my legs and arms, making walking with a cane even difficult; and, the associated muscle weakness, lack of coordination and inability to control how my muscles were moving, all made sense to me now. Working out at the gym was becoming more of a difficult task each and every day. Earlier in the book, I suggested that I would soon have to make a decision if I wanted to maintain my quality of life, and it now looked like several decisions would have to be made in the very near future.

Throughout my childhood and adult life, sports and exercise played a large part in my life. They were an important aspect of who I was, and were a distraction to the nuances of everyday life. Along the way, my faith took a back seat while I was searching for what made me, me. Throughout my life, I had my low and high points, and what I have found from coping with my illness, is that God will never leave my side, through the tough times, and the not so tough times, and when we need to make those decisions that will impact our lives for the foreseeable future, I remind myself in these times of trials and tribulations, to put myself in God's hands—and watch.

October arrived on "schedule" and the month would prove itself to be a time of more change. I was now six months off chemotherapy and my MRI once again showed a decrease in the tumor. At this time, the neuropathy in my left side had taken its toll, and, Nancy and I purchased the wheelchair we both knew was an inevitable circumstance in my life, and, I had to suspend my gym membership. Contemplating these changes and where I go from here, I began searching within myself, and had the chance to really take a hard look at my life as it was now. I believe that God works his way into your life without you knowing it, to prepare you for the challenges that may face you.

For me and others diagnosed with glioblastoma, searching for answers is a common thread we share, I believe God has a way of getting our attention, and we find ourselves wanting Him in our life. Having a diagnosis of glioblastoma is certainly an "attention grabber." In these times, I accepted God into my life and it would never be the same again. Changes in your life are never easy and sometimes seem impossible to overcome; a scripture in the Bible served as a source of encouragement for me: Jesus replied, "What is impossible with man is possible with God." (Luke 18:27) I now look upon each day as a work of art in progress and try to live each day, each breath as if tomorrow is a gift and not always a guarantee.

November arrived with no surprises and on the 13th I turned 55 years of age. Another milestone, and I realize now that life is not a sprint, and not to rush life, and witness the miracles around me.

Nancy and I, along with her sister, attended the "Race for Hope" walk/run in Philadelphia to fight brain cancer. The staging point of the event was at the steps of the Art Museum which I thought was clever of the organizers. If you remember the movie "Rocky," Sylvester Stallone used the steps as part of his training, symbolically representing the formidable challenge he was facing. Like me and others with a cancer diagnosis, facing our challenges, there is always hope when you allow hope to be available to wash away the despair. With the help of Nancy and her sister taking turns pushing me in my wheelchair, I was able to complete the "walk."

As the year 2008 came to a close, I believe I came out of the year a better, stronger person, ready for the new challenges in my life, with Nancy and God by my side. In my distress I called to the LORD; I called out to my God. From his temple he heard my voice; my cry came to his ears. (2 Samuel 22:7)

Chapter VI

My journey thus far has been filled with good times as well as bad times, and there were certainly times that tested my spirit. As I look back, I believe my diagnosis allowed me a second chance at life; would I have preferred a different path, most definitely. In life we must play the hand we are dealt, and as I mentioned earlier, God has a plan for us. Throughout my walk, my renewed connection to my faith helped me through these changing times, and having God by my side had given me the spiritual conviction to move forward. Without this, living with terminal cancer I believe, would have been like a blind man feeling his way through a lifetime of darkness.

January 1, 2009, a New Year, and I was certain new challenges in my life. I was now ten months off chemotherapy and I was still having some digestive issues requiring additional procedures to ascertain the problem area; these symptoms would continue for a few months until rectifying themselves. This, along with the neuropathy I was experiencing, sometimes zapped my mental and physical energy. I would be continuing my bi-monthly MRI schedule and the anxiety preceding them had diminished some, but it was always on my mind, "is this the one." It was also a time to rebound from the emotional roller coaster I had been on since my diagnosis. Accepting what I had to deal with overtime, made me realize that self-pity would not allow me to mentally challenge this fatal diagnosis; the psychological effects of coping with glioblastoma can be equally as devastating as the physical effects.

My "mantra," for the New Year, was to live each day one at a time, and not to look over my shoulder too long, because there was so much life still waiting for me to experience. I earlier described life as a book by God's design with many chapters, and if I did not "turn the pages," I would not experience the next chapters in my life. This would be particularly true if I became mired in my diagnosis, and did not allow myself to seize upon the opportunities life presented me every new day.

On March 1st, I "celebrated" three years of *living life* and was looking forward to the onset of spring. My MRI once again showed a decrease in the tumor and was almost barely visible on the MRI scan. I have been fortunate to this point, and know that many others diagnosed with glioblastoma have not been so fortunate. Although my MRIs have continued to show a decrease in the tumor, I remember being told by my neurosurgeon in 2006 that at some point in time, I would more than likely need another surgery to remove a "recurrent tumor." My MRIs did not necessarily mean that the tumor was being completely destroyed, but only that it had decreased in size.

Despite my physical and cognitive "handicaps," I continued to engage in what activities I was able to manage. With the aid of my wheelchair, I was able to go to outdoor flea markets, something that Nancy and I continued to enjoy. I was reading a little bit more than before, but I was still having difficulty keeping pace with the contents of a book especially one's that involved multiple characters, dates and locations. It took me several weeks to finish a book which I would have read in days before my diagnosis.

Throughout April and May, Nancy and I were able to visit the shore and share relaxing moments on the beach, go to our favorite flea markets, and attend support group meetings. The following months were unremarkable, other than my routinely scheduled MRI and attending a Cancer Survival Day event at the hospital where I was initially treated in 2006; it was a "slow" few months considering everything.

During this time Nancy and I began watching my daughter's Maltese named "Bentley;" we pretty much "adopted" him. Having him around and engaging in antics with him helped me fill some of the day when MRIs and doctor appointments did not fill the calendar. I was now fifteen months off my chemotherapy and other than the numbness I was experiencing, I was none the worse. We continued going to the beach as much as we could, and I enjoyed the tranquility of just watching the wave's crash onto the beach, listening to children laugh, and watching seagulls frolic in the water, as Nancy walked the shoreline looking for beach glass. My scheduled MRI was on the horizon, and the anxiety level usually associated with this event, no matter how routine it had become in my life was always a bit unnerving what the results may revealed.

I was relieved to read that the MRI showed no change in the tumor from the previous MRI. Although I had become accustomed to my MRIs showing a continual decrease in the tumor, "no change" was equally as gratifying. With every MRI, came with the anticipation that this "may be the one" that shows a recurrence of the tumor, or, new tumor growth. Any anxiety I may have had before each MRI was never at a high level, but concerning. If an MRI showed a recurrence of the tumor, I knew I would be in a lot of trouble, based on my experiences with members of the support group who were diagnosis with glioblastoma, and had recurrent tumors; it was not a desirable situation—most died within months after their surgery. Other thoughts that I had before each MRI were what would I do? What would my options be? And where would I go to have the necessary surgery.

I tried not to think about these issues but rather "relax" within the confines of the MRI apparatus and listen to my music. I always enjoyed listening to music and made it part of my therapy as a way to "escape" the mundane schedule of MRIs and follow-up doctor appointments. I made it a point to leave at least one hour of my day, to enjoy the comfort music brought to my life.

My August MRI once again showed "no change" from the previous one, even though this was the second MRI that did not show a decrease in the tumor, I reminded myself to be thankful for the progress that I have made up to this time and to take each day one at a time, and not to get ahead of myself—"no change" was a good thing.

September and October were relatively "quiet" months. We celebrated two birthdays, Nancy's and Bentley's. We also attended each month's support group meetings. On October 18th, the quiet was broken by the news that my Aunt had passed away. She had been in a nursing home over the past few years due to a stroke she had suffered, and I was fortunate enough to have the chance to visit with her along with Nancy and Bentley just a few weeks before her passing. I had very fond memories of her; I spent a lot of time with her and her children (my cousins Frank and Donna) on my grandparent's farm during the summer months when I was a young boy—she will be surely missed.

November ushered in another year of my existence—another milestone, another miracle. On the 13th I celebrated my 56th birthday, and, I was now nineteen months off my chemotherapy, and coping with the "minor" deficits of my illness. Compared to what other support group members diagnosed with glioblastoma were facing on a day-to-day basis, I was doing well. I tried not to over think the "casualties" in my life brought on by the cancer that invaded my brain. I remind myself that life does not always give us what we hope for, and observe what the LORD your God requires: Walk in obedience to him, and keep his decrees and commands, his laws and regulations, as written in the Law of Moses. Do this so that you may prosper in all you do and wherever you go. (1 Kings 2:3)

Over the course of attending support group meetings, I was approached by some of the wives from the support group, who were caring for their husband's, diagnosed with glioblastoma. They asked me to speak with their husband's who were having a difficult time coping with their diagnosis; I always found the time to find a little humor in life, despite my diagnosis, and shared this humor at the support group meetings. Perhaps that is what attracted them to me for support. I eagerly acquiesced to their requests, and found myself in a position to possibly help someone navigate their course. Some, not all, were having a difficult time of it; anger, pity and a mindset of death, pre-occupied their thoughts. This mind-set of suffering could be understood when prevailing statistics tell you that you will more than likely die in the near future.

When I met with these men individually, I would suggest to them that despite the dire statistics there have been cases of long term survival, and that everyone is their own "statistic of one," and there is no reason to believe that they cannot be one of those cases that go beyond median survival. I would remind them of the positive's in their lives; their wife, children, family and friends who cared very much for them and still needed them in their lives, and unfortunately, some of these men passed away within months.

On a few occasions, Nancy and I were able to socialize a few times with one of the couples who lived close by. We met for lunch, and had enjoyed each other's company. Sadly, the husband passed away soon after our last outing together. He passed away 7 months after his diagnosis, and there would be many more to follow. In a 6 month span of time we (the group) lost another 6 members diagnosed with glioblastoma; one of whom was a 4 year survivor who developed new tumor growth.

December was a month of several snowfalls—some small, some with accumulating snow. My MRI showed no change from the previous—"no change" is a good thing in the glioblastoma world. No new growth and stable ventricles are also comforting news. My mind wanders sometimes, and thoughts that I may really have a chance at beating this awful disease, fills my head, and it is now becoming a battle of wills—mine against my formidable foe. I do not fool myself into believing that I can "outwit" death, but until that day comes, I will rely on God to chart my course, and deliver my fate into his hands; from God we learn to live.

Over the course of my diagnosis there have been many cliques used to describe me while I was living with this horrific cancer on a day to day basis; some say I am "courageous," others, refer to me as a "hero." I am neither; I am just a simple man, doing what I can to live life while I live. I often tell those individuals, that Nancy is the true hero in all this, and without her and my faith, I would not be where I am today; "God made my life complete when I placed all the pieces before him, when I cleaned up my act, he gave me a fresh start. Indeed, I've kept alert to God's ways; I haven't taken God for granted. Everyday I review the ways he works. I try not to miss a trick, I feel put back together, and I'm watching my step. God rewrote the text of my life when I opened the book of my heart to his eyes." (2Samuel 22:21-25)

Chapter VII

January 1, 2010, and I am now twenty-one months off chemotherapy, and have a 6 mm tumor (barely visible on the MRI), stable ventricles, and no new tumor growth; what more could I have hoped for?

Despite the available medical literature describing glioblastoma as ultimately fatal in months, not years, gave me hope that it was possible to survive longer than the survival statistics predicted. Albeit, some members of the support group diagnosed with glioblastoma succumbed within the median survival range, I remained positive in my rationale that we are all a "statistic of one" and that each of us will have our own story-line. This was the "catch 22" with the support group; we shared our stories, our fears, and formed bonds of solidarity only to sometimes lose a new found friend.

Despite a positive MRI days earlier, I found the need to go to the emergency room. I had been having a series of headaches over the past few days, and growing more concerned, that they were not my "normal" migraines I suffered through during the winter months, and the fact that they were not dissipating made my decision for me. As it turned out, a cat scan showed no irregularities relative to my brain tumor. An intravenous "rush" of morphine did the trick to relieve the pain. February turned out to be another month of snowfall and my MRI once again showed "no change."

On March 1st, I reached the unthinkable; four years of living life with the deadliest of malignant brain tumors. Thoughts on continued fortune were not on my mind, and I was focused only on today, and where do I go from here. I surmised over the past few years, that being diagnosed with glioblastoma and surviving for years beyond the prevailing median survival range was pretty much the "luck of the draw." Each individual will have varying results with their treatment, and for me, maintaining a positive attitude and believing in myself and my faith went a long way to strengthen my resolve to live, laugh and love throughout my days as I continued to move forward with God by my side every step of the way; "There is surely a future hope for you; and your hope will not be cut off." (Proverbs 23:18)

April was a significant month in my journey; it marked two years since I stopped my chemotherapy treatment. The treatments I had started four years ago brought positive results and my tumor "friend" was fading, and no new "friends" were knocking on my door. I do not consider myself "lucky," but rather fortunate. Luck has no measure of credibility when it comes to glioblastoma; there were many others, not so fortunate. The side effects of my treatments thus far have been adaptable and I have learned to balance my life with these changes, and find the "positives" that are around me everyday.

My April MRI remained unchanged, the tumor was barely visible and the ventricles remained stable. Despite this, I would continue to remain cautiously optimistic—living with terminal brain cancer is like living in a shadow of darkness; you never know what is going to jump out at you.

Over the past month, I was still experiencing sharp pains in my pelvic area. As I described earlier the urologist was reluctant to proceed any further than giving me pain medication and a six-month follow-up visit. Future visits had the same results—continue medication and a six month follow-up. In the interim, I had an especially painful experience that required me to make an "emergency" visit to my urologist. At the time, he was not available and I was referred to his partner—this visit was a "train wreck" from the moment I met with him, it seemed that I was taking up his valuable time—he reviewed my chart and basically reiterated what his partner noted in my chart—he recommended follow-up in six months. By now, it seemed apparent to me that they were intimidated by my brain cancer, and were unwilling to perform a standard procedure to correctly diagnose what I was experiencing. I would also find this to be the case with other physicians outside my cancer care. After this visit, I made a decision to seek out another urologist, and, at the very first appointment, he recommended the procedure known as a *cystoscopy* to determine what I was experiencing with my bladder—my first thought was: at last.

The urologist explained that a cystoscopy involved the insertion of a tube like object with a small camera attached to it through the shaft. The thought of this was more disturbing to me, than the thought of having my skull cut open the night before my craniotomy. Go figure. He continued that because of the male anatomy, the bladder's location can only be accessed by this method. The fact that I would be awake during the procedure only heightened my anxiety. A 10mg valium prescribed by the urologist got me through the procedure. My bladder showed no sign of disease, and it was determined that the pain I was experiencing was due to an enlarging prostate, typical with my age, and it was pressing against my bladder. The urologist recommended a treatment of medication to "relax" the prostate to alleviate the pressing against my bladder. It was his opinion that a biopsy of my prostate was not necessary at this time based on a physical examination and blood tests (PSA). I would be seen again in 6 months.

June arrived and we were looking forward to spending time at the shore. My MRI once again showed "no change." I was now eight months from reaching the elusive five year term of "living life." As I mentioned earlier, an article published on glioblastoma cited estimates that only a "handful" of glioblastoma patients will reach this term of survival. From the very beginning of my diagnosis, I navigated the unknown terrain of living with a high grade malignant brain tumor, and the early months of successful results, encouraged me, and brought about a realization that I continue to embrace: that statistics are just numbers and that I am the only number that matters.

July and August were typical New Jersey hot and humid months that limited my time outdoors—it was difficult for me to remain outdoors in either very hot or cold weather since my diagnosis; I had become very sensitive to both weather conditions. My MRI once again showed "no change" that delighted my neurooncologist. My faith and a belief in myself, to overcome these challenges in my life helped me find the motivation to take the first step of each new day, no matter how small, and appreciate the day God has given me as a gift, filled with opportunity, beauty and joy. While reading the Bible, I came across an inspiring set of words dealing with adversity in one's life: "My soul finds rest in God alone; my salvation comes from Him. He alone is my rock and my salvation; He is my fortress, I will never be shaken." (Psalm 62:1-2)

September and October were months of routine follow-up appointments with my neurooncologist, and urologist, and another MRI, which once again showed no evidence of recurrence, new growth, and stable ventricles.

The effects of the peripheral neuropathy were now taking their toll on me. I also became gluten sensitive, and prone to urinary tract infections. I "appeared" to be functioning normally on the outside to friends and family, but what they could not see, was what was happening on the inside; this would be a continuing theme throughout my *sojourn*. I have come to a conclusion that people see and hear what they want to see and hear, and disregard the rest. This became very frustrating at times, for me and others, I am sure, diagnosed with any type of brain tumor.

During a scheduled visit with my neurooncologist, we discussed my MRI schedule. On my previous visit, we had a conversation on the possibility of having my MRIs every three months, instead of the two month schedule I had been on since my diagnosis. At the time, he said he wanted to wait and see the results of my October MRI. After reviewing the results, he gave his "ok." Although it would be nice not to undergo as many MRIs, I did have some reservation as I did, when I discontinued my chemotherapy treatment; I took that "leap of faith" that if there were a recurrence of the tumor, it would be identified when it was in its infant state, and more susceptible to treatment. I did not look at this as a life or death decision, a recurrence of the tumor at any time would result in the same decision making process. As I wrote earlier, it had been my experience with some support group members who had recurrent tumors, passed away shortly thereafter. December was bringing to an end my fourth year of living with the glioblastoma, and ushering in the challenges I may face going into my fifth year.

Life is just so unpredictable; we never know what is around each bend in the road, over each hill, and around every corner. We all face new challenges in our lives each and every day, regardless of our physical state of being. How we cope with these changes in our life will determine how we proceed going forward; life does not wait for us to catch our breath for too long, it moves on with or without us. Looking back can certainly have its benefits; it gives you a template on which to set your compass, the trick is, not to get stuck in the quagmire of the past; learn from the past to live a better future. The following is a scripture passage that I believe helped me. (I Samuel 2:6-10):

> The Lord brings death and makes alive; he brings down to the grave and raises up. The Lord sends poverty and wealth; he humbles and he exalts. He raises the poor from the dust and lifts the needy from the ash heap; he seats them with princes and has them inherit a throne of honor. For the foundation of the earth are the Lord's; upon them he has set the world. He will guard the feet of his saints, but the wicked will be silenced in darkness. "It is not by strength that one prevails; those who oppose the Lord will be shattered. He will thunder against them from heaven; the Lord will judge the ends of the earth. "He will give strength to his king and exalt the horn of his anointed."

Chapter VIII

From the very beginning of my diagnosis I was often approached by family and friends to create a *bucket list* of places I wanted to see, and "things," I would like to have. Without actually saying it, the implied suggestion was, these were moments and things I should *take with me* before I died. I politely listened to their suggestions, and in my mind, dismissed them without a second thought; "damn the bucket list" was my attitude. Creating a "bucket list" in my mind, was accepting death now, and giving up on living life on my terms. My rationale was, when the end comes, it will come, and I did not need to go "mountain climbing" or, "bungee jumping" from tall bridges. What I needed was to set a foundation on which I could build a future no matter how long that future might be. To achieve this, I used the following verses from the Bible, "Proverbs" as a template to establish the foundation of living my life:

> "Hope deferred makes the heart sick, but a longing fulfilled is a tree of life." 13:12;

> "The fear of the Lord is a fountain of life, turning a man from the snares of death." 14:27;

> "The path of life leads upwards for the wise to keep him from going down to the grave." 15:24;

> "A cheerful look brings joy to the heart, and good news gives health to the bones." 15:30;

"To a man belongs the plans of the heart, but from the Lord comes the reply of the tongue." 16:1;

"A cheerful heart is good medicine, but a crushed spirit dries up the bones." 17:22;

"A man's spirit sustains him in sickness, but a crushed spirit who can hear?" 18:14;

"The name of the Lord is a strong tower; the righteous run to it and are safe." 18:10; and

"The tongue has the power of life and death, and those who love it will eat its fruit." 18:21

From what I have experienced over these past years, life doesn't always cooperate with you—it often lulls you into a false sense of security—offering expectations only to be dashed by circumstances beyond what we could imagine; changes in our life that will alter how we live, and our ability to live the life we wanted not so long ago.

Throughout my journey, challenges and the changes brought on by my diagnosis was a focal point in my survival up to this point in time. One of the most frustrating aspects of these changes was how I was perceived on the outside, by others. I looked perfectly "normal," and if you stood me along side anyone else in a room, it would be hard to identify who was who—it is what was going on the inside that could not be seen by others. Family and friends wanted so desperately the "me" they were accustomed too, because I was able to function at an adequate level, they were often disappointed when I could not join in activities I normally would have engaged in. Without knowing it, they pushed me to the point of frustration, and I would ask myself: "Why don't they understand, I can only do what I can do." This same frustration was frequently echoed at support group meetings; some members shared all too familiar encounters with friends and outside entities. I will not use their names but only refer to them as a "member."

While discussing this issue at one particular meeting, a member revealed an incident they were involved in weeks earlier. On the way to work, they were involved in an incident with their vehicle. The member called the police, and when they arrived, the officer began questioning the member about the incident, and quizzed the member about their sobriety; an affect of the member's brain tumor was slurred speech and the officer construed from the slurred speech that she was under the influence of alcohol. As he continued this line of questioning, frustrating the member to the point where they actually showed the officer the scar where their craniotomy was performed. Eventually the incident was resolved and the officer apologized that "they got off on the wrong foot." A suggestion was made by several members that "we should carry some type of card issued from our physician that we are brain tumor patients."

Still, another member related a story involving them and a person they were dating. This individual and the member had dated at one time prior to their diagnosis. It was several years later, that they ran into each other again, and began dating. Because of the medication they were taking, the member was prone to personality shifts which led to "heated moments" in the relationship. The member could not understand why the individual did not grasp what they were going through, leading to added frustration for both of them. I suggested that it would be an unfair expectation on our part to place on others to understand our situation without having the knowledge we have; how can they? Instead of frustrating one another, I suggested that they sit and discuss what was going on with their brain tumor and some of the side effects associated with their medication. Knowledge is understanding, and understanding leads to constructive communication; people need to talk with one another, not at one another. I have also had my own personal experiences with this issue; friends and family at certain times seemed to be ambivalent about the changes in me brought on by my diagnosis. I realize now, that perhaps I placed an expectation on them, and should not have expected anything less.

I believe expectations and hopes are two different realities in life: Expectations are a belief that an outcome <u>will</u> occur, and hopes are a belief that an outcome <u>may</u> occur. At the beginning of my journey I had both hopes and expectations of what may lie ahead of me. My journey with glioblastoma certainly did begin with the expectation of death, and now, it is a path of hope which has allowed me to know the differences between what I can change in my life, and things I cannot:

> God grant me the serenity
> to accept the things I cannot
> change . . . . the courage to change
> the things I can . . . and the wisdom
> to know the difference. (Serenity Prayer)

My faith, I believe, had given me the insight to look for a deeper meaning in my life, outside the opinions and beliefs of others, and provided me with a purpose and a foundation on which I could build upon through the rough times in my journey. By putting myself in God's hands, I surrendered myself to his will; the simple words of prayer say so much, and encouraged me to always love the moment I am in, and the drive to seize these moments. I do not have a crystal ball; my doctors do not have an oracle that they consult. Faith and hope are all we have. To believe in ourselves is to know ourselves. I think I know who that person is staring back at me in the mirror, and sigh knowing the image is but a shadow of my former self. I had to get to know me, who I am now, and not recede into the shadow of my former self.

Anyone coping with a terminal illness, like me, eventually will find themselves at heavens gate, to get there, I walked through the *valley of the shadow of death*, and straddled the abyss of life and death and hoped to come out the other end in one piece, alive:

> The Lord is my Sheppard; I shall not want
> He maketh me lie down in green pasture; he leadeth
> me beside still waters.
> He restoreth my soul; he leadeth me in the paths of
> righteousness for his name's sake.
> Yea, though I walk through the Valley of the Shadow of death,
> I will fear no evil for thou art with me; thy rod and thy staff
> they comfort me.
> Thou preparest a table before me in the presence of
> mine enemies; thou anointest my head with oil; my
> cup runneth over. Surely goodness and mercy shall
> follow me all the days of my life; and I will dwell
> in the house of the Lord forever.
>
> Psalm 23

Chapter IX

By this time in my journey, I had experienced many loses and overtime, these loses became less of a concern as I focused on the growth of my spiritual self—the power to survive, derives from your soul. As these loses mounted one on top of the other, I sometimes became frustrated over these changes in my life. During these times I reminded myself to be grateful for what I have in life, and not to feel sorry for myself. Although everything was not perfect in my life, I had to adjust to these loses in my life.

I now use plastic utensils to eat because metal still leaves an unusual taste in my mouth;

I can no longer wear any type of jewelry made of metals; gold, silver or any type of composite, not even my prescription eye glasses because of the metal wire inside the arm of the glasses;

I can no longer place any type of cologne on my skin without irritating me; this included, any type of scented shampoo, body wash or soap;

I can no longer run, ride a bicycle, swim or engage in any type of physical activity involving coordinated motor functioning; to walk very short distances I need the use of a cane and to cover long distances, I need the use of a wheelchair.

I find it difficult to eat the foods I once enjoyed, due to acquiring gluten sensitivity and digestive problems. I now have acute urinary tract infections that are usually treated by antibiotics;

I cannot hold long conversations, or read as much as I would like to, due to cognitive issues associated with my brain tumor; and can not be in a crowded room with a lot of people talking at the same time without having the sensation of a radio station being too far from its tower;

I no longer drive a car due to safety concerns associated with my diagnosis.

To help me stay focused on the now in my life, and not what was, I have found these "verses" maintain my focus, and help me stay on a positive direction. I call them the "steps" to overcome the challenges I encountered.

- My strength to overcome challenges I face, comes from my tenacity to live life;
- The growth of my spiritual self transcended the survival of my physical being;
- There were no dark moments in my life that could not be healed by faith;
- An inner acceptance that death is part of God's plan for everyone;
- Caress the moments that God has presented to me, and cope with the changes in my life that come my way;
- Allow each day to bring love and laughter into my life;
- To believe in the strength of my faith to serve as my inspiration to do what I needed to do to live life on my terms;
- To always take the time to discover the miracles around me, and not be distracted by the maladies of my illness;
- To always love the moment I am in;
- To follow God's path no matter how many times I am knocked down, and get up to face my challenges;

I sometimes find that not so long ago, my life was not so complicated. I awoke in the morning, went to work, solved my problems and returned home—it was a very simple life. It only became complicated when I made it complicated. I am, by my very nature, my own worst enemy at times. Living in these turbulent times, notwithstanding, my glioblastoma diagnosis I still wanted to achieve a sense of comfort for myself, my daughter and Nancy. With so many paths to choose from to achieve what I believed brings happiness, I sometimes complicated the tiniest matters:

> When there is food on the table
> there are many problems. When there is
> no food, there is only one problem.
>
> *(Chinese Proverb)*

As I have said several times, the ability to maintain my direction in these times of trials and tribulations came from my inner strength, my will, and my center. It allowed me to focus on my horizon and detach myself from any anxiety, and grief I associated with my diagnosis. Just as I was my own worst enemy at times, I overcame these self-inflicted attachments by a higher level of understanding, and the power to heal myself spiritually and physically.

The element of faith and inner strength encompass what I would describe as the spiritual matrix of my existence. When I was only consumed with thoughts of not surviving my diagnosis, I could not see the *forest but for the trees*; when my mind became so preoccupied with my fate, I failed to see the beauty that surrounded me, the ordinary, sunrises and sunsets that God made for me. When I separated myself from these thoughts of despair about my fate, my mind became free of suffering and I was able to witness the most beautiful entities that I once took as ordinary occurrences. If your mind is not free of your suffering then even the most beautiful entities in your life do not seem so beautiful. As a terminally ill cancer patient, I have probably subconsciously experienced this at one point-in-time on my journey. For example if I allowed myself to become angry or sad, then even the most beautiful rainbow over the horizon looked ordinary. The most important thing I could do for myself, was to keep my mind focused on the positive entities in my life, which some may feel is impossible to do when your mind is racing and filled with anxiety about what your next MRI may reveal.

Throughout this narrative, I have attempted to emphasize that our inner strength, our soul, and our faith are the foundation to overcome adversities that happen upon us; they are our center. If we lose these puzzle pieces, we lose the ability to see life for what it is; when you keep a strong determined outlook you can see things as they are, and not as they once were.

I have mentioned on several occasions that my faith is the foundation of my existence. It allows me to challenge adversity, and a "rock" to cling too in the most difficult times in my life. One of my favorite inspirational readings reminds me that God is always with me in those most difficult times, is *Footprints*:

> One night a man dreamed he was walking along the beach with the Lord.
>
> As scenes from his life flashed before him, he looked at the path of footprints and noticed that during the saddest times in his life, there was only one set of footprints in the sand.
>
> Troubled, he asked "Lord, why did you leave me when I needed you most."
>
> The Lord replied, "During your times of trial when you see only one set of footprints it was then that I carried you."

Faith can be defined as simply believing in something that we can not see or touch. I feel most of us reach out to God when overwhelmed with diversity whether it is cancer, or other issue(s) in life. When we hit "rock bottom" it is then when we often turn to our faith.

I would like to recognize the "un-sung hero" in my life for everything she endures on a day to day basis being my copilot; keeping me in control of my life, and helping me navigate the challenges I face. As my caregiver, Nancy shared the same anxieties I experienced. She too, had to develop her own coping mechanisms as she watched me cope with a glioblastoma diagnosis; it was through her strength and courage that I was able to sustain myself and avoid the pitfalls of depression, self-pity, and a mindset of suffering. No matter how hard I pushed, she did not fall and always stood tall. Looking back over these past years, I can only imagine how difficult my diagnosis had been on Nancy's psyche. She was there from the very beginning, and never wavered in her love and devotion for me; she set aside her needs, to tend to mine. I always appreciated this sacrifice as the days turned to months and the months into years. Nancy and I have always been candid, and continue too be, about my diagnosis. From the very beginning we were both caught up in the madness of what a glioblastoma diagnosis would mean to our lives, and what would lie ahead of us, and the individual struggles, we would both be challenged with. We now accept my diagnosis as an everyday challenge to overcome and try not to make it an everyday focus in our lives.

As I continued to live beyond what was expected, my survival remained a mystery. Although I have lived beyond what was expected, the physical, emotional, and cognitive changes brought on by the tumor and treatments, were constant reminders of what I was living with.

My passion for living life to its fullest has often labeled me as an inspiration for others to follow. I do not consider myself an inspiration; I am just doing the best I can under the circumstances I am living with. I believe we all inspire one another to be the best we can be, and to look upon others coping with challenges in their lives as a "spark" to ignite the fire within them.

When I think of where I started and where I am now, it is hard to believe how quickly life moves on with or without us.

Chapter X

"For there is a proper time and procedure for every matter though a man's misery weighs heavily upon him. Since no man knows the future, who can tell what's to come? No man has power over the wind to contain it, so no one has power over the day of his death. As no one is discharged in time of war, so wickedness will not release those who practice it." (Ecclesiastes 8:6-8)

Throughout time there have been many essays and treatises on the subject of death written by both eastern and western philosophers. So too, for those of us affected with a terminal illness, and for those fortunate souls not dealing with this issue in their life; death is as different as night and day—I know death personally, and those not afflicted with a terminal illness, only know death as a casual acquaintance. The prospect of death is with me everyday, it is my shadow; it circles my life like a predator stalking its prey. For others, death is surreal, it has no substance, no feeling, and no emotion, it is an abstract phenomena.

Over time, I have accepted that people cannot relate to me on this subject. Perhaps being told you will more than likely die from a diagnosis within months, not years leaves you thinking about your own mortality one dimensionally rather than in the abstract. When I was first diagnosed, the thought of death did not frighten me as much as the thought of leaving the people I cared about—what would they do without me? These thoughts were with me thru the day and night time hours, when it was first inferred that I would most likely die much sooner than later.

I have read many passages on how everyone should have the opportunity to "live life like they were dying." I do not particularly ascribe to this variation of living life; one should live their life no matter what their situation is. How I chose to engage in life prior to my diagnosis, was a choice of free will. I would like to share some prayers that I feel may inspire others to take each new day in their lives and turn it into something special. If we allow life to take us for a ride, and unburden ourselves from the everyday problems life can present, you need not be dying to have meaning in your everyday life "let your faith be your guide."

-Let Faith Be Your Guide-
Prayer from the heart

If we want to find a deeper meaning in our lives we have to go to that place within ourselves.

> O Little flower of Jesus,
> Ever consoling troubled souls
> with Heavenly Graces,
> In your unfailing intercession
> I place my confident trust.
> From the Heart of our Blessed
> Saviour
> Petition these blessings of which
> I stand in greatest need.
> Shower upon me your promised
> roses
> of virtue and Grace, dear
> St. Theresa, so that swiftly
> advancing in sanctity and in perfect
> love of neighbor, I may someday
> receive the crown of Life Eternal.

O most holy heart of Jesus, fountain of every blessing, I adore you, I love you, and with lively sorrow for my sins, I offer you this poor heart of mine. Make me humble, patient, pure and wholly obedient to your will. Grant, good Jesus, that I may live in you and for you. Protect me in the midst of danger; comfort me in my afflictions; give me health of body, assistance in my temporal needs, your blessing on all that I do, and the grace of a holy death.

May the roads rise with you, and the wind be always at your back;
And may the Lord hold you in the hollow of his hand.

I shall be there to listen to your cries, your sadness.
I shall be there to cure your grievances, your misery, your sufferings.
Mary is, and shall always be the Mother of all mankind.
We must heed Her call to love and obey Her Beloved Son.

> "O Mary, conceived without sin,
> pray for us
> who have recourse to thee".

Praying the Hail Mary with the following jaculatory prayer we save many souls and earn grace for ourselves and for our families. The prayer of the Flame of Love Include the following request in the prayer you say in her honor, the Hail Mary:

Hail Mary, full of Grace, the Lord is with you. Blessed are you among women, and blessed is the fruit of your womb, Jesus. Holy Mary, Mother of God, pray for us sinners, now at the hour of our death. Amen

Mother, flood the whole humanity with the blessing of your flame of love. Amen

A Healing Prayer to St. Jude

Most holy Apostle, St. Jude, friend of Jesus, I place myself in your care at this difficult time. Pray for me; help me know that I need not face my troubles alone.

Please join me in my need, asking God to send me consolation in my sorrow, courage in my fear, and healing in the midst of my suffering. Ask our loving

God to fill me with the grace to accept whatever may lie ahead of me and my loved ones, and to strengthen my faith in God's healing power.

Thank you, St. Jude, for the promise of hope you hold out to all who believe, and inspire me to give this gift of hope to others as it has been given to me. Amen

St. Anthony, Saint of Miracles

O Holy St. Anthony, reach down from heaven and take hold of my hand. Assure me that I am not alone. You are known to possess miraculous powers and to be ever ready to speak for those in trouble.

Loving and gentle St. Anthony, reach down from heaven I implore you and assist me in my hour of need. Obtain for me (mention your request)

Dearest St. Anthony, reach down from heaven and guide me with thy strength. Plead for me in my needs. And teach me to be humbly thankful as you were for all the bountiful blessings I am to receive. Amen

-"Feel faiths power"-

No matter what life threw at me on my walk, I would always remember that God would never leave me, and He would be with me through the best of times and the worst of times. I believed that He would never leave me or forsake me, this sense of security allowed me to get out there and enjoy the beautiful creation He made for me everyday. We never know what life will throw at us, and I am happy to know that God will surely help me carry my cross in times when I feel I am not strong enough to overcome the trials in my life. If we believe, faith can certainly "move the mountains in our lives."

We all want a better tomorrow, the chance to heal whatever is broken in our lives and the hope of a future to do both. No matter what the challenge I faced, I found that special something in my life that inspired me, and energized my resolve to live life everyday and find new meaning in my life; a purpose—that purpose God planned for me. With faith and hope, hand in hand I awoke each morning facing the uncertainties of tomorrow; where hopes and expectations can be so easily crushed. In these moments I would recall the Bible scripture (Isaiah 45:6-7) "So that from the rising of the sun to the place of its setting, men may know there is none besides me. I am the Lord there is no other."

This is the way God helps us through our times of trial—he presents us with another day, filled with new opportunities. What I mean by this, is, that no matter when we feel we are separated from life either in the spiritual or physical sense, the earth will continue to rotate on its axis and bring a new dawn. It is up to us to rotate on our spiritual axis to find the miracles that are with us everyday, and allow each dawn to bring us another *opportunity* to create a better situation for ourselves.

Everyday, we are all faced with challenges in our lives; having a diagnosis of any kind of cancer can be both physically and mentally exhausting. As I continue to live, the challenges of my diagnosis, and the challenges of life in general, sometimes feels like a "double whammy;" God reminds me in his own way, "*Let not your heart be troubled;*" the unforeseen, unexpected, circumstances in our lives, represent those tiny pieces of time that we cannot predict or manipulate. As difficult as it may seem, moving forward with hope, was a challenge of unexpected success when I delivered myself from my past. Everyone goes through life expecting something back—life doesn't always cooperate and give us what we hoped for, but what we didn't expect. This is especially true for those of us afflicted with a debilitating illness that has changed our life.

I could not think of a more unexpected "challenge" in my life, when I was diagnosed with brain cancer. Prior to my diagnosis, I moved through life as though I were stuck in a tunnel, halfway in and halfway out, and nowhere to turn. I lost my vision, and sometimes a belief in myself to create a better situation for me. Throughout this book, I have focused on my faith—my *inner strength* to create beyond what I could have ever imagined; I reminded myself every day, to live life to its fullest and appreciate all the tomorrows God has given me.

While doing research, and perusing many articles about glioblastoma, I came across many stories of individuals struggling with a malignant brain tumor diagnosis. The most disheartening of these stories were those of children diagnosed with pediatric cancer. Soon after, I began donating to St. Jude's Hospital and every month or so, I receive a newsletter and read about the hardships the parents endure, as well as those innocent children; it made my situation seem small. I had the opportunity to experience many moments in my life that these children will never witness in their lives. I believe that when people afflicted with any type of illness, who, begin to feel self pity for themselves, should read the stories of these children and their courage to overcome the adversary in their lives.

As human beings we all experienced times in our lives when we became lost, when life just wasn't cooperating with us, and there seemed to be no end in sight to our suffering. It is in these times God was listening. If we allow Him to enter our lives, and become our copilot, He will offer you a path of hope: I will lead the blind by ways they have not known, along unfamiliar paths I will guide them; I will turn the darkness into light before them and make the rough places smooth. These are the things I will do; I will not forsake them. (Isaiah 42:16)

I often compare ourselves too a puzzle made up of many different pieces, and that each piece makes us who we are, and that these pieces fill a particular aspect of our life, and take on many shapes and sizes; that life is not a "one piece" fits all puzzle—that there is no secret to one's true self, you just have to feel it, trust in yourself, and believe in yourself as God intended: "In his heart a man plans his course, but the Lord determines his steps." (Proverbs 16:9)

Tethered with faith and hope, and a better understanding of myself, I forged ahead and faced the challenges in my life head on; I woke each morning and faced the mundane issues of solving problems, attending to domestic matters, paying bills, and scheduling daily activities (for the most part Nancy burdened the load, and I offer what assistance I could). Life is a vacuum my amigos; it sucks us in no matter what our circumstances are, and the only choice we have is to maneuver ourselves to the best of our ability, and our spiritual constitution. There were times when I looked back at what life was like prior to my diagnosis, and at the time it seemed to me that beginning on the day of my diagnosis, I had no past—my life has been what it is today—there was no yesterday.

Over the course of my diagnosis, Nancy and I would sometimes wonder where some of the people that we were once close to, have disappeared too. I suggested to Nancy that most, if not all friendships, are based on a *commonality* between them, and once that thread was no longer there, the friendship begins to dissipate; this was the case with some of our former friendships.

Earlier, I had described the last day I was able to participate in golf with some friends of mine. I did not know at the time, it would be the last time I would see them. My friends and I had been golfing together as a "foursome" for nearly fifteen years. Over that time, we never socialized with each other outside playing golf together, and when golfing season was over, we went our separate ways for the winter and reconnected again in the spring week before the start of the new season. What kept our friendship together over those winter months year after year was the commonality of our friendship—golf.

For most everyone outside "my world," life is lived at a "sprinter's pace," while mine is a marathon. I look back at moments in my life and ask myself: "did I take the time to witness the special moments in my life." My point is we must adjust to our particular set of circumstances, and stay engaged in our life, without expectations of ourselves and others in our lives; we all step to the beat of our own drum.

When I first waded into the murky unknown waters of my diagnosis, expectations and hopes were abound. My naivety, and childish innocence, gave way to the stark reality of my predicament and the dire statistics associated with surviving my illness. As I suggested earlier on, statistics are just that, numbers; they do not reveal the spirit of the individual; me, my spirit, was the only statistic I needed to be concerned with. Yes, there were some that passed away within the median survival range, and others were marginally more successful in surviving. And yet, others like me who achieved much more beyond what was expected; it was God who determined my destiny, and I walk the path He has planned for me without expectations, just the hope He provides for everyone each and everyday.

You see my friend, we just don't know; either do the entities that gather these statistics. As I mentioned earlier, physicians do not have an oracle to consult with and tell us how much time we have left, they rely on statistics to determine the expected longevity for those of us diagnosed with glioblastoma.

In closing, I thank you for reading my story as well as Bruce's, and remind you to take time to appreciate the minutes and hours each new day brings—we can't always have what we want in life, do not extinguish the light within you, and never give up without a fight in anything you feel worth fighting for. God is our refuge and strength, an ever-present help in trouble. Therefore we will not fear, though the earth give way and the mountains fall into the heart of the sea, though its waters roar and foam and the mountains quake with their surging (Psalms 46:1-3) And now these three remain: faith, hope and love. But the greatest of these is love. (1 Corinthians 13:13)

> "If it shall be that I have no tomorrows, I want to see you swing through the door, laugh and sing, and have that one last fling.
>
> I want to see you on your feet, dancing to life's beat, and partying all thru the night under the moonlit skies; listening to the ocean's roar, and feeling the sand under your feet.
>
> I want to see you in the street, walking in the rain, and feeling no more pain."
>
> Stephen Hatrak

God speed and always remember to live, laugh and love all the days of your life.

A Story of Survival and Overcoming Challenges

As I mentioned earlier in the book, there are other stories of survival with person's diagnosed with non malignant brain tumors. This is one such story in his words:

> *Some folks tell me that my story is beneficial to them.*
> *I don't know about that (!), but here it is:*

It was 1994, and I crawled under my car for some repairs. I had to stop what I was doing—I suddenly got very nauseated—attributed (I thought) to a recent bout of the flu. Next, the fingertips on my left had started to tingle. I figured they would stop on their own. Instead, (over a few months), the fingertips on my right hand started tingling . . . Then, I noticed that at nights, I wasn't swallowing, and would slobber on my pillow (This was DISGUSTING!!!). I would awaken each morning with a terrible headache (really, my upper neck). This was solved by taking three extra strength Tylenols, and lying on the couch for 1/2 hour. Every once in a while, I would cough badly (because I used to smoke cigarettes). When this happened, I would become VERY dizzy, and everything would go black, I would almost pass out. I found out later that this was from "hydrocephalous," the build up of fluid on the brain. I remember driving on the highway at this time—I had a coughing fit. I knew what was coming, and realized that I just couldn't black out while driving on the highway. I remember screaming out loud, "No! No!!!—It passed, and I did not black out. God was there. My vision was doing some strange things—I was diagnosed with "vertigo" (incorrectly). I got out of breath very easily—sometimes just when standing still. People noticed me staring off into the distance with a blank look on my face for 20 to 30 minutes . . . I could no longer take our dog for walks. I wouldn't play outside with the kids . . . Once, I was sitting on the "Throne" (commode) one night . . . I felt everything go black, and fell to the floor. Although totally awake, I could not move a single muscle. After five minutes or so, I was able to pull myself to my feet and stagger back to bed . . .

So—why didn't I go to the doctor? Well, I did. I was misdiagnosed for a period of two years. I was in the military at the time, and went to the local base clinic. I have to accept some of the blame—even if a PA (Physician Assistant) told me that nothing was wrong with me, I KNEW there was, and I should have pursued the matter further. In retrospect, I suppose I was afraid of the reality. I knew something was seriously wrong, no matter what I was told. I took a "stress test," where they plug you up with many wires attached to your body, and I was to walk on a treadmill. The technician had me lying flat while he applied the wires—which ran to a computer. He told me, "OK, stand up, and run on the treadmill for X number of minutes." When I stood up, his monitor went "nuts." He told me to sit down, and then got 3 doctors to come and see. They did, and the test was halted. These 3 I really blame—they SAW that there was a real problem, and neglected it. The PAs who are not fully trained doctors (yet), just didn't know better. I went to one complaining of all of my major symptoms. He told me we would deal with "one at a time," which made sense to me, but was wrong. He should have looked into what was causing all of the problems. This went off and on for two years, as I already wrote. Then . . .

I had a seizure. I was at home, on my couch. I flopped about, and vomited on myself. All of this was in front of my poor son, who was just a child at the time. I didn't hear his calls to his mother. She ran into the room, scared to death, just as I was coming "to." This was the "straw that broke the camel's back." She cried to me that I just "wasn't right" anymore, and I had to go to a real doctor NOW! I went to the clinic, and since it was on a weekend and there was no doctor around, I saw another PA. He told me that since I had not urinated on myself, that it was not a seizure. The following Monday, I was back at the clinic, this time to be seen by an MD. I demanded the best they had. When she called my name in the waiting room and I staggered toward her, she knew something was seriously wrong with me. She called another MD in to the exam room. They both did tests on me, then spoke to each other in hushed tones. She sent me to an off base diagnostic center that had an MRI machine. That test was performed—I returned to the base with my scans in hand. She looked at them for a bit, then sat Shirley and me down . . . "I have some bad news . . . You have a brain tumor. You are NOT to drive anywhere, which is a DIRECT ORDER. Be back here at 1800 hrs (6:00) for an ambulance ride down to Bethesda Naval Hospital. They have a brain surgery department there. You will be on medical leave for three months" . . .

After I was ambulanced it Bethesda, Maryland, I immediately entered the "National Naval Medical Center" emergency room. In a few minutes, a doctor (my neurosurgeon) came up to me. He did a very brief examination, then asked me, "where's your family?" I told him that they were back in New Jersey—the kids were in school, and we didn't want to take them out and disrupt their studies. His next remark made the gravity of my situation apparent, "get them here." He then turned and walked away.

Zoom ahead to the day of the surgery (the next day)—because I don't remember anything in between. I do recall being on a gurney, and being wheeled into the operating room. The anesthesiologist approached me with a mask for the gas. He asked, "Are you ready?" He then jumped up on my back, and clamped the mask over my mouth, very hard. He did not immediately turn on the gas—I had nothing to breathe! My last recollection was of me fighting this guy for my life . . . He must have turned on the gas, because I went out . . .

I was then laid face down on an operating table. The surgical site was prepared. Surgery took 13 hours (or so I am told). My wife was updated hourly. While happy to be kept informed, she later told me her heart "stopped beating" whenever that phone would ring. Surgery was performed by two neurosurgeons. They wore microscopes that helped them see the minute differences between the tumor and the healthy brain tissue. Ultimately, over 99% of the tumor was removed. I have since tried to contact these doctors to update them on my still being alive after all of this time. But as is the case in the military, they have long since moved to other bases, and I cannot locate them.

I awoke in intensive care. Tubes went in my mouth. I was groggy. My Father told me, "You did good!" I thought, "No, the doctor did good—I was asleep!" I stayed in ICU for a week. Some interesting things happened . . . I was wheeled down to get an MRI. I fell asleep—if you have ever been in an MRI machine you may find this hard to believe—lots of banging, clanging, etc. My sister told me what happened another time . . . a nurse made her "rounds," and gave me morphine in my IV. Then, she either forgot to annotate her actions on the chart, or the next shift of nurses misread it, because I got ANOTHER dose! I was extremely stoned—to the point that I even asked for a pen and paper and asked my sister if I could borrow her car! I am told now that such a "double-dose" could have killed me . . .

Don't try this at home . . . I remember this one well. I had a "morphine moment" where I thought that there had been 22 tubes down my throat, and they took out 21, but forgot the last one. So, I took it out for them! I remember how when I had the thing halfway out, that I probably shouldn't be doing this. But, I couldn't shove it back down—I might damage something in there . . . so, I took it out and handed it to the nurse . . . I remember her screaming, "Doctor! . . . Doctor!!!" The next thing I recall, I was waking up again with the tube back in my throat, and my hands tied to the bed! It had been my breathing tube, without which I would have suffocated.

What a sight! I had the big breathing tube in my throat, a feeding tube in my nose, and a catheter in my . . . well, you know. My vision was terrible—everything was double. (Still is). I was confined to the bed—no way could I walk (yet!). I could not eat, I had no swallow reflex. I was fed through a tube that was first in my nose, then through one that went directly through a small slit in my skin directly into my stomach. I couldn't talk—not with the breathing tube in. So to communicate, I was given a board that had the alphabet on it. I was to point to the proper letter and spell out my message. This would be maddening slow in itself—but with my double vision, I kept pointing to the wrong letters. My wife wondered just what in the world I was trying to say—I usually gave up in disgust . . .

After a while (I have no idea how long), the decision was made to remove my breathing tube and see if I could breath on my own. They did, I remember taking short loud gasps for air. My doctor told me, "calm down and try to breath normally" I REALLY tried hard. But—I woke up with a trache tube cut into my throat. It was for breathing—still, I could not talk . . .

I then moved out of ICU and into a "regular" ward. I had an IV, a "pulse oximeter" (that measures the oxygen content of your blood), a catheter, a PEG (feeding) tube, and these really cool stockings (NOT socks!) that were supposed to eliminate the formation of blood clots. They failed, but I'll tell you about that later . . . I had an oxygen tube going into my nose. And, my pajamas were three sizes too big! Those and my stockings made quite the fashion statement . . .

Now that I was in the "regular" ward, things happened fast. It was determined for me that since less than 100% of the tumor was removed, I would need radiation treatments. They would be administered at another hospital in the D.C. area—Walter Reed. My days were pretty full, with this doctor and that one poking their head into my room, testing this or that. I remember being annoyed at these interruptions—all I wanted to do was sleep!

One doc came in. "Who is the president?" (I got that one wrong . . .) "What was D-Day? What is your name? Your wife's' name?" All sorts of neato things for me to "peck" out on my alphabet board. Although I had the trache in, it wasn't "plugged;" the result was that I could not talk. I was helped to a lounger chair to sit in. While in bed, the nurse put my sneakers on me so my feet would not go flat. My mother had told me that I had better NEVER lie in bed with my shoes on. Boy, if she was here, she would be MAD!!! One day, a doctor came in to tell me he was "downsizing" my trachea. Big deal—it still felt the same! About a week later, they plugged it up completely—to see if I could breathe on my own. It worked—I could talk. The speech therapist asked me if there was anything I wanted to say to Shirley . . . I croaked out, "I love you" (WooHoo—points!!!) My voice really sounded terrible—I surprised myself!!! I sounded 150 years old . . .

I had daily speech therapy sessions, where they not only worked on my speech, but my swallow and gag reflex. This lady had a glass of ice that she would chill a spoon in, and then put it in the back of my mouth. I did not gag, I did not swallow. It was just there. I was annoyed, I wanted to sleep . . . Eventually, I had a "barium swallow," where I had to eat this radio-active substance called Barium, while standing in front of an X-Ray machine. That way, the docs could watch and see if I was swallowing completely or if some was going into my lungs (a bad thing). I failed miserably. More feedings through the PEG tube in my belly . . . Two weeks later, I had another

Barium test—I passed! The tube was removed, and I was put on a regular diet. Hospital meatloaf has never tasted so good!!! Mmmm!

In speech therapy, I had to speak into a microphone which went into a computer. When looking at the readout, my therapist mentioned that mine was the most "messed up" test she had ever seen! Croak on!!!

Psychologists came to my room to see how depressed I was (I wasn't, and they never came back). I was taken to physical therapy one day—I was laid flat on a "bed" and had to learn how to sit up all over again! (I was pretty bad off) Weeks later, again in physical therapy, I had to walk about 10 feet, while holding on to these railings for balance. I tried so hard—concentrating completely on each step . . . Finally, I noticed people were laughing at me, pointing at me. My wife had a look of horror on her face. I looked down. There, around my ankles were my PJ bottoms . . . no wonder I was having so much trouble walking! Of course, I had nothing on underneath. Strange—that wasn't as important as making it to the end of my walk! I pulled up my drawers, and kept trying! Whatever!!!

I stayed in this hospital for about one month. All of my family had to leave to get back to work, etc. My wife and kids also had to leave—they returned home so the kids could get back into school. They had already missed a whole month. I assured everyone that I would be fine, and off they went. *note—this was VERY hard on Shirley. But, I assured her I would be fine. In a few days, I was taken by ambulance to Walter Reed.

The ambulance ride to Walter Reed was uneventful. I arrived OK, but the Naval folks sort of forgot to send my medical records with me . . . it was just me!!! I was shown to my room. It was determined that a doctor would have to do a physical on me. This pretty young female came into my room, and told me, "OK, take your clothes off." I told her I would, but she had to first . . . then she told me she was a doctor! (I didn't know—hey, I just had brain surgery!!!)

Walter Reed constituted the second part of my treatment—and would be my home for two months. Many different treatments happened there. I had radiation treatments, physical therapy, occupational therapy, speech therapy. All sorts of infections happened there. (Not that it was a bad place—the care was top notch. My infections would have happened anywhere). While at Walter Reed, I saw many other patients, some way worse than me. This gave me strength; it made me realize that I wasn't so bad off. That was one of the most important things I learned—you can't get any better if you are dwelling on the severity of your current situation. So in a very real way, those very ill folks performed an important task that they never even knew they were doing . . . .

At this point, I was confined to a wheelchair. This was my first exposure to such a device. As I sat in it for the first time, I tried to wheel away. It felt difficult to wheel on the left side . . . I guess my left arm had weakness—from the tumor or the surgery. I had seen little old ladies wheel themselves around . . . there was no way I wouldn't be able to do the same thing. So, I "toughed" it out . . . . A WEEK later, I found that the brake was on (duh!). I removed the brake—life instantly got better! I moved to a walker for a short while, then to crutches. (To this day, I keep a cane handy—my balance isn't the greatest . . .)

Physical therapy seemed useless . . . I had to wheel myself down there, wait the usual 10 to 15 minutes, and then get to ride a stationary bike for 10 minutes . . . Or, I would get this exercise or that one. What a waste, I thought . . . actually these things worked! I still can't dance, but come to think of it, I never could (!) Life went on this way. I would have daily radiation treatments . . . where I had a special mask made out of plastic mesh that was heated, and laid on my face to conform itself. Once put on and strapped to the table, I couldn't move my head. That way the radiation would be EXACT. The beam of radiation is many times more intense than an average X-Ray. Its purpose is to destroy any tumor cells remaining. Unfortunately, it also damages good tissue along its pathway. Both of my ear canals became inflamed and tender—and now years after treatments, I still have problems with my ears that require medical attention (I have an appointment next month . . . Until then, I will be hard of hearing out of my right ear, and there will be this loud "ringing" . . . Oh, well—at least I am alive to complain about it!) My hair fell out in the back of my head. When it re-grew, it came in a few shades lighter. Does it look good? Who cares—I don't have to look at it—that's YOUR problem! There were many somber faced folks in radiation oncology. I finally realized that they had CANCER!!! Pathologically, my tumor differed from cancer only in how it looked under a microscope. So—mine was benign—Thank God! (I have since had many friends with "benign" tumors die . . . any time something grows in a confined space such as the skull—it is a BAD thing)

My weekdays were taken up thusly—this appointment today, that one the next day. Most just broke up the drudgery and boredom. Radiation treatments can cause many unpleasant reactions in people. In my case, I just got tired . . . . It seems I was always tired!

One day during a slack time, a nurse wheeled me outside to get some sunshine and fresh air. It was a beautiful spring day—she pointed out a robin . . . . I broke out sobbing! Now, I had no connection with the bird—I actually had no idea why I was sobbing. But—let me tell you, I was doing some big boo-hooing! Tears and everything! I found out later that some folks that have just had a surgery can bawl at times. So, although I was sobbing, I was also laughing. How strange! (That nurse NEVER took me for a walk again!!!) ***Note—this also happened to my friend David (angel now) at his daughter's bat mitzvah (or however you spell it). She was about to be honored in this solemn ceremony, when her dad busted out in uncontrollable laughter. He wouldn't stop, some of the audience politely chuckled, although they didn't know why! After the "bird" incident, I was allowed to go home on the weekends, providing I was back in place next Monday morning. This single allowance helped me SOOOOOO much. I will ALWAYS be indebted to the members of my military squadron who volunteered to drive the 4 hours to D.C., and the 4 hours back home. It was on one of these trips back home when I noticed my hair was falling out. Now—what do you do when you are in someone's car, with a handful of hair? I'm sure they wondered why I was opening the window—it was still cold outside!!! I tossed the many handfuls of hair out . . .

Up till this time, I would have my many appointments Monday through Friday, and then just watch TV Saturday and Sunday. BORING!!! But going home made me feel more like ME—although I usually slept the whole weekend, I got to see my wife and kids. My doggy remembered me!

One week before my surgery, Shirley and I picked out a house we liked. We got a VA loan . . . . Their red tape dictated that the loan could only be approved to an alive veteran, so (I still love this) I had to make the statement "I am Bruce Blount, and I am not dead." This was witnessed by an officer, annotated, then faxed to the V.A. Shirley had to close all by herself. While signing the many papers, my wife was told that there was an outstanding warrant for her arrest. With my frightened wife reduced to tears, she received an apology; she was evidentially not the same Shirley Blount—who is a black woman, and my wife is white. She composed herself, and continued signing. I came home to our new house. Life was looking up.

"Why is your left leg so much bigger than your right one?" My doctor (the pretty one) asked one day. "I have no idea" was my reply. I had noticed pain there, all that day. The nurse told me it was probably due to my not walking too much . . . .

I was taken to ultrasound—where they "looked" into my left leg. More hushed words, then the familiar tone of voice, "I have some bad news . . . ." I had a blood clot in my leg. The big worry was that it could dislodge, travel to my heart, then to my lungs, killing me. Oh, boy . . . . Treatments were to either chemically dissolve the clot, or install a "Greenfield Filter" in my Vena Cava next to my heart to catch the thing, should it dislodge. The doctors were hesitant to use the dissolvers, as it might have impacted the healing of my surgery. So, I now have a titanium filter in my chest. This doctor "snaked" it through my vein—from an incision in my groin. "A Little Pinch?" It hurt like hell! After a few, he said, "all done". I was told to lie on my back, and not move for 24 hours. Wonderful Let's see—I also had pneumonia which was treated with drugs. I contacted a urinary tract infection—a high fever and all—more drugs . . . I lost a total of 30 pounds while in the hospital. I later joked that I had invented the "Brain Tumor Diet", and was going to get rich!!!

Later, in my bed, a doctor checked on me. I wasn't asleep although he must have thought I was—my eyes were closed. He said, "Poor guy, everything has gone wrong for you."

Optometrists there prescribed "Prism" glasses for me. They (pretty well) corrected my double vision. Up till then, I wore an eye patch, and resembled a pirate . . . AAARGH!!! To this day I have to wear prism glasses. This is OK; they look just like regular glasses.

The day came when I had my last radiation treatment. Speech therapy was finished. So was occupational therapy. Eventually, the day came when I was set free!!!

It was almost three months to the day since being diagnosed. The military had little use for someone unable to run (barely walk), with extremely poor balance, double vision, and extremity weakness—I was told that I would be "boarded out" of the Air Force. This was fine with me—my priorities had changed so much . . . . It took a whole year, but I was medically retired. Did I end up with a 100% disability rating? Nope . . . .

The next few years were comprised of me learning the "new me." But—I got bored with "me," and decided to go to college. I did well there, earning a 3.45 grade point average. Then came Algebra. What a disaster!!! I have never tried anything so hard in my life! I took notes (3 notebooks full)—I got a tutor. Nothing worked—I failed the course. Not once, or twice . . . I took the same course three times. Each time I failed. I just could not remember those little "squiggles" . . . I went to my school counselor, and told her about my problem with my memory. She scheduled a meeting between me and the school doctor—I was going to try and get a waiver for math. I met the doc—he had a suitcase full of little wooden blocks and such. He tested me for an hour, then told me, "I don't see a problem . . . I don't think you are trying hard enough." I am usually very calm, but my blood "boiled" when he said this! I told him, "maybe your little test does not work for a brain damaged by a tumor" . . . I got up and left the room . . . The end result is that I do not have a degree.

One day, I "Googled" the words "brain tumor"—and clicked on a link to something called T.H.E. Brain Trust. Within that organization, I found an online support group for adult ependymomas. I went there, and wrote to the facilitator that I was a survivor, and would be willing to help others however needed. She added me to the group. About one year later, she asked if I would take over for her. I did, and to this day I remain at the position of facilitator. I like it, and have gotten many "thank you's" which mean everything to me! I have made friends there that will be in my life for as long as there is life in my body!

I also co-facilitate the Monmouth and Ocean County Brain Tumor Support Group here in New Jersey. The people there are my friends—I love the connection with them!

There are other things I have accomplished—which I will mention, but not go into detail. (I dislike people who brag!).

I have been to Washington, D.C., acting as a brain tumor activist. While there, I spoke to elected officials and their staffs about BTs. I have written an article that was published in a local newspaper (BTs again). I have requested (and gotten) a proclamation from my mayor declaring the first week in May as "Brain Tumor Awareness Week." Probably my greatest achievement was being highlighted on CNN.COM. After that, I was written about by three local newspapers, and honored by my mayor. I have spoken at one conference, and am scheduled to speak at another in a few months.

So—did I ask for the tumor? Of course not. But, I'll say it again—I have said it before. (This one is sure to anger some of you)—"I recommend a brain tumor as long as it does not kill you." My life has purpose now. I appreciate each and every second I am alive.

EPILOGUE

Today I am none the worst from what I described throughout this narrative. On March 1, 2011 I celebrated five years of living with my diagnosis and in December we attended the "Voices against Brain Cancer Walk/Run" in New York's Central Park along with my sister Joan, her husband Earl, my daughter and two of my nieces, Samantha and Georgia. Nancy continued to be my inspiration, and we continued going to the beach as much as we could. We still enjoyed going to outdoor flea markets and attended as many support group meetings as possible. Bentley continued to be our constant companion.

On March 1, 2012 I celebrated my sixth year of living with glioblastoma multiforme. My daughter is now working in the banking industry and attending graduate school working towards her MBA.

Looking back, my plans were simple—playing golf as much as I wanted, hanging at the beach all day a few times a week over the summer months and perhaps even taking up surfing again. This was my plan after retirement. Sometimes, "the best laid plans" do not come to fruition.

My diagnosis of glioblastoma just a few short years from my planned retirement date dashed those dreams; my golfing days would now be an occasional visit to the golf course, vicariously playing golf through the people I was watching.

My days of hanging at the beach, taking long walks along the shoreline with Nancy, would now be limited to a few days a month in the early morning hours before the heat of the day took its toll on my body. My strolls along the shoreline are now strolls on the boardwalk with Nancy and my wheelchair. Despite these turns of events the majesty of the ocean and the serenity of the golf course landscape still bring a sense of enjoyment into my life. My oars maybe broken and my sails a little tattered, but I still charter my course forward with Nancy and my faith as the mast upon which I set my sails.

What I expected did not appear, but the miracles that surround me, however, did not disappear. These miracles inspire me not to lose faith in myself. Faith is a belief in things when everything around you tells you not too. I build upon these miracles that have been made for me and to find the message that each new day presents itself with.

My journey was laden with many hurdles only to be faced with other trials ahead of me. I navigated these misty waters the best I could with few expectations. I cannot hide from what I cannot see; like the ocean, vast and wide, and unforgiving in its fury at times, the cancer that invaded my brain created an ocean of shadows of "what once was and will never be."

I appreciate the consequences in my life as they serve as a reminder to live life to its fullest, laugh as much as life allows, and find the message of hope that each new day will present me with. It is said that there is a silver lining in any trial endured. Receiving God into my life and embracing the wonderful people I have met on my walk has certainly been a blessing beyond what one would expect—my silver lining.

> Only be careful, and watch yourselves closely so that you do not forget the things your eyes have seen or let them slip from your heart as long as you live. Teach them to your children and to their children after them.
>
> (Deuteronomy 4:9)

You came near and stood at the foot of the mountain while it blazed with fire to the very heavens, with black clouds and deep darkness.

(Deuteronomy 4:11)

But if from there you seek the Lord your God, you will find him if you look for him with all your heart and with all your soul. When you are in distress and all these things have happened to you, then in later days you will return to the Lord your God and obey him. For the Lord your God is a merciful God; he will not abandon or destroy you or forget the covenant with your forefathers, which he confirmed to them by oath.

(Deuteronomy 4:29-31)

Nancy and Me
May 28, 2011
Manasquan beach

Printed in Great Britain
by Amazon